Xtreme Business System (XBS)

AUTHOR: Dr Michael J Freestone

PUBLISHER: MJF GROUP

Copyright Notices

Copyright © 2020 XBS

No part of this publication may be reproduced or transmitted in any form or by any means, mechanical or electronic, including photocopying and recording, or by any information storage and retrieval system, without permission in writing from the Publisher. Requests for permission or further information should be addressed to the Publishers.

Legal Notices

While all attempts have been made to verify information provided in this publication, neither the Authors nor the Publisher assumes any responsibility for errors, omissions, or contrary interpretation of the subject matter herein.

This publication is not intended for use as a source of legal or accounting advice. The Publisher wants to stress that the information contained herein may be subject to varying state and/or local laws or regulations. All users are advised to retain competent counsel to determine what state and/or local laws or regulations may apply to the user's particular situation or application of this information.

The purchaser or reader of this publication assumes complete and total responsibility for the use of these materials and information. The Authors and Publisher assume no responsibility or liability whatsoever on the behalf of any purchaser or reader of these materials, or the application or non-application of the information contained herein. We do not guarantee any results you may or may not experience as a result of following the recommendations or suggestions contained herein. You must test everything for yourself.

Any perceived slights of specific people or organizations is unintentional.

Contents

Copyright Notices 2
Legal Notices 2
How To Use The Extreme Business Systems XBS Program? 8

XBS Module 1 11

The XBS Business Growth Principles 11
21 Business Building Concepts to Make A Business Strategically Unstoppable 11
Introduction 12
XBS Principle 1 13
XBS Principle 2 14
XBS Principle 3 15
XBS Principle 4 18
XBS Principle 5 20
XBS Principle 6 21
XBS Principle 7 24
XBS Principle 8 28
XBS Principle 9 33
XBS Principle 10 35
XBS Principle 11 36
XBS Principle 12 37
XBS Principle 13 38
XBS Principle 14 40
XBS Principle 15 43
XBS Principle 16 45
XBS Principle 17 47
XBS Principle 18 48
XBS Principle 19 49
XBS Principle 20 50
XBS Principle 21 51

XBS System Module 2 52

Fast Cash Tactics 52
8 Fast Cash Tactics to Flood Your Business with Money Now 52

XBS Module 3 Lead Generation 68
Getting an Endless Supply of High-Quality Leads for Your Business 68

XBS Module 4 Niche Marketing 71
Multiply the size of your business by targeting specific people and businesses that have a perfect need for your product or service 71
Introduction 72
   Stage 2: Your Own Company Analysis 81
   Stage 3: Identifying Possible Niches 84
   Stage 4: Choosing The Perfect Niche 85
   Stage 5: Defining Your Chosen Niche 87

XBS Module 5 89

Unique Selling Proposition 89
The second most important thing you must do to grow your business is to construct your own "Unique Selling Proposition" – get this right and your targeted prospects (your niche) will not be able to resist your product or service! 89
   Introduction 90

XBS Module 6 96
The benefits you provide are important to your prospects and clients or customers – benefits are what they are buying

....96

XBS Module 7 106
Module 7 Risk Reversal 106
One of the few marketing tools you can use instantly to multiply the size of your business overnight! 106

The XBS Programme 119
Module 8 Fonts 119
Making your advertising and marketing communications easy to read to ensure the highest response 119
   Introduction 120
Module 9 Testimonials..127
Helping you generate many more leads, by proving you can deliver on your promises! 127
   Introduction 128
Module 10 Irresistible Offers 137
How to multiply your sales and profits using irresistible offers 137
   Introduction 138
Module 11 148
Lead Generation Strategy 148
How to maximise your response (and minimize your costs) by carefully matching your lead generation tools to your target or niche market(s) 148
   Introduction 149
Module 12 154
Setting Your Objectives To Give You Direction 154
Creating objectives to give you a sense of tremendous satisfaction and to help drive your business forward 154
   Introduction 155
Module 13 Budgeting...156
How to set your initial lead generation budget, and why you'll never need to budget in the future 156
   Introduction 157
Module 14 162
Selecting Your Lead Generation Tools 162
Choosing your lead generation tools and putting in place your 'Marketing Activity Plan'..........................162
   Introduction 163
Module 15 166
Testing is the simple way to get the best possible results for the least time, effort, and cost 166
   Introduction 167
   Conclusion 174

Welcome

Welcome to the 'Xtreme Business System (XBS).

In this program, you'll learn everything you need to know to create your very own business building system based on the most effective and radical business growth Tactics available to any business. Better still, we're going to show you how to put these Tactics on auto-pilot using the Xtreme Business System (XBS).'

Never before has a program been made available that shows any business owner how to put in place a series of amazingly powerful Tactics and then successfully systemize each strategy to ensure you get repeatable results over weeks, months and years.

Why We Created This Program For You

The purpose of this program is to give you step-by-step, practical instructions you can apply immediately to your business, so you too can build a successful business in the shortest time possible.

There are many books and theories about how to 'market' businesses. But most of them fall well short of their goal. They tell you what to do, but only give sketchy details on how to actually do it. And they concentrate on 'traditional' sales and marketing techniques – many of which don't work for most businesses.

And they NEVER tell you what to do first, what to do second, what to do third…

This program will concentrate on the three necessary components for developing a phenomenally successful and profitable business:

> 1. What to do
> 2. Why you're doing it
> 3. Precise step by step details of how to do it

Of these three components, Step 3 is the most important. We believe the reason that most businesses fail or at least fail to grow at the rate they should, is because they lack the simple skills and basic know-how of the things that make a difference.

Never before has someone been able to say with true conviction that if you follow "these steps" you will be more successful. That is until now!
And why should we be any different?

The XBS Program is a system you can follow irrespective of what business you're in or what product or service you sell. It's a system that leaves nothing to chance. Follow the system and we guarantee you'll grow your business with massively increased profits.
Anything is possible when you apply the Tactics, we'll be revealing to you. Yes, it does take effort, but the great thing about the XBS Program is this…

Once your XBS is in place it virtually runs by itself. You'll keep generating leads and enquiries and keep converting them into high quality customers, or clients. And you'll keep selling and reselling to existing customers or clients. The process works so you don't have to think about it.

What You'll Get from The XBS Program

We've designed this program to give you all the 'what to do,' 'why to do it,' and 'how to do it' information you'll need to make your own business as successful as possible.

Our basic philosophy is that success can be 'modelled.' We know this works. Together we've grown, or been instrumental in growing, literally hundreds of businesses all over the world using the very same time- tested Tactics you're about to discover. And hundreds (now thousands) of other businesses around the world are also getting the same great results using this program.

Better still…

We've given you every secret, every principle, every strategy. No details have been spared or missed out. And you get the lot – well all the stuff that works!

Not one aspect of the information contained in this program is theory. None of it is hearsay. None of it is based on concepts. Everything you read has been tried and tested.

Plus…

None of the marketing secrets, principles and Tactics contained in the program require you to do any 'cold calling.'

And it couldn't be easier.

As long as you follow the Step-By-Step XBS Modules as we've laid out, everything will come together in a logical and sensible order. We can't stress to you how important this is.

We've made it as simple for you as possible. Just follow the step by step instructions in each XBS Module – then turn to the Workbook (at the end of each Manual) to complete your own strategy, and you'll create an amazingly powerful business growth system.

The scale of your success is not down to us – it's down to you. We've given you, and will give you the proven tools, which if applied will rapidly grow your business. Nothing worth achieving is easy. But with some effort on your side you really will see some jaw dropping results.

Okay, now that you understand where you'll be going, and what you need to do, let's get started. But first let us say one more thing.

We're extremely excited about this program. We believe it is the only program of its kind anywhere. We don't know of anything else that's as comprehensive, practical, and as proven as this program is for business owners and entrepreneurs.

So welcome aboard. And may your business become far more profitable than your most optimistic projections!

How To Use The Extreme Business Systems XBS Program?

The XBS program has 4 separate (but interlinked) Manuals…

MANUAL 1: Setting Up Your Lead Generation System (Current offering)

MANUAL 2: Setting Up Your Sales Conversion System, Implementing Tactics to Increase Sales and Profits From Existing Customers, And Improving Profit Margins

MANUAL 3: The Quantum 133 Tactics and Action Points That Can Revolutionize Your Business

MANUAL 4: The Master Copywriting Course

Each Manual is sub-divided into two easy to use sections. Here's how to use both sections to get the
best possible results:

SECTION 1: The XBS Modules

The XBS Modules guide you through the whole XBS. This is your step-by- step 'blueprint' that you
must follow in a logical order to get the best possible results.

Each XBS Module contains examples showing you how the strategy has been used, complete with step-by-step instructions of how you create the strategy for your own business.

Don't skip any XBS Module. You'll see from a very early stage that the XBS Modules are intertwined, dependent on each other, and require a set order for you to get the optimum results.

We've arranged the XBS Modules in the most effective order so you can put in place your own XBS with the least time and effort on your part. Start missing or jumping Modules and you'll make life harder for yourself!

SECTION 2: The Workbook

After each XBS Module, you need to turn to the relevant section in the Workbook (located at the back of each Manual) to complete the Module.

It's vital you do this to ensure you diligently apply each XBS Module to your own business by following the simple step-by-step instructions.

Before we get started you first need to see how the XBS Program fits together...

A Simple Overview of The XBS Business Tactics Program

Below is the diagram showing you the simple system that makes up the XBS Program. This is what your own XBS will look like once you've finished...

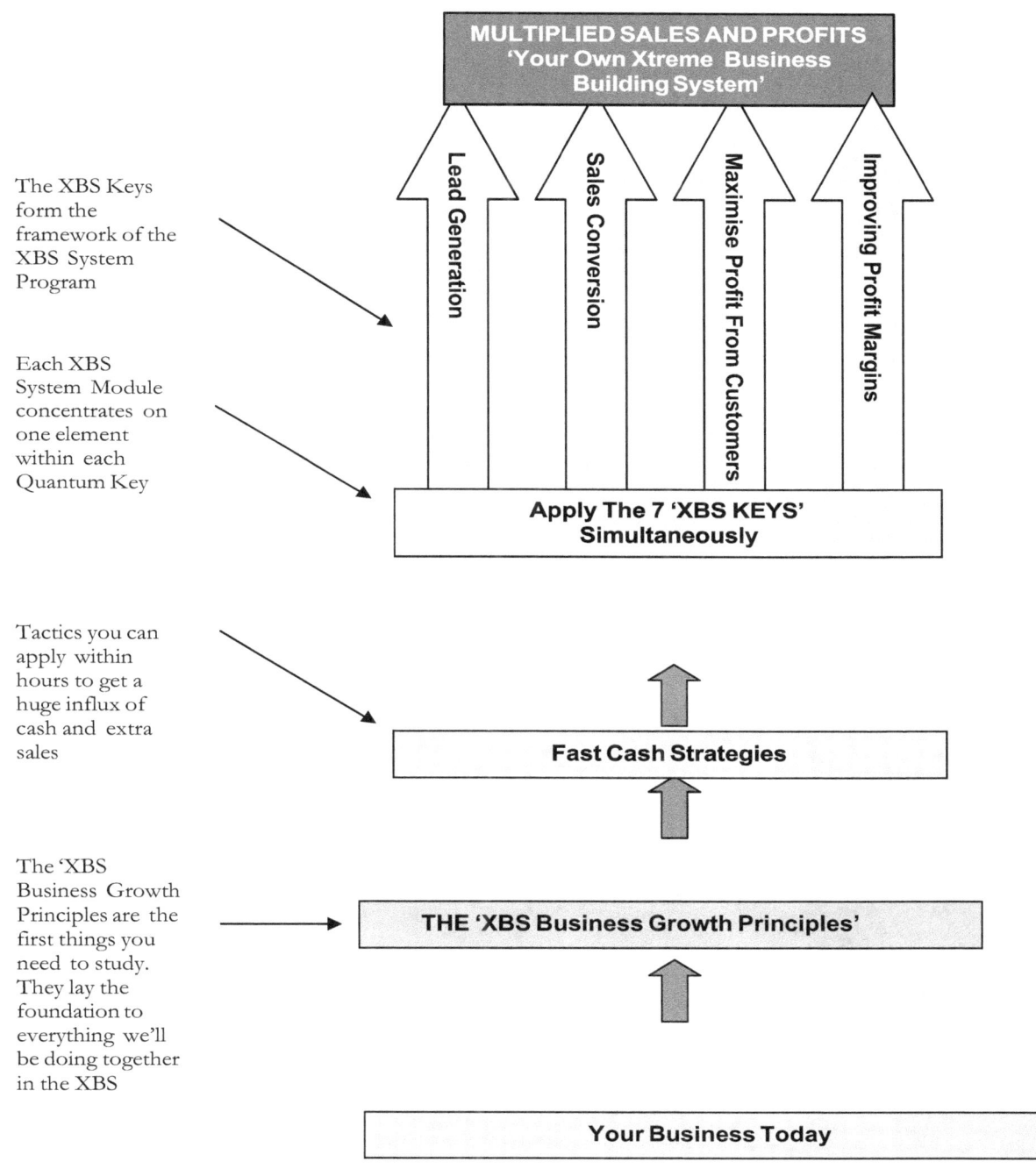

That's the XBS System Program shown as one complete and seamless process!

Your journey begins with the XBS Business Growth Principles. That's what we'll first be focusing on…

XBS Module 1

The XBS Business Growth Principles

21 Business Building Concepts to Make A Business Strategically Unstoppable

Introduction

In this first Module you are being introduced to the most exciting, powerful, and profitable business building principles in the World.

These dynamic concepts are not part of the traditional marketing approach talked about in conventional marketing and business books or taught in the Universities. Instead they form part of the 'street wise', 'common sense' and 'guerrilla tactics' marketing school, proven time and time again, to provide you with an 'unfair advantage' over your competitors. The application and implementation of this information into businesses, has over the years made billions upon billions in newfound profits.

These same principles make up the foundational knowledge base of The XBS Program.

As you can see from the diagram on page 8, the 'principles' are the foundation to everything we do. So, everything you do from now on will follow one or more of these principles.

Perhaps the easiest way to explain how the principles work in conjunction with everything else you'll be doing is to give you a very simple example…

Let's say you decide to use advertising in newspapers or magazines as one of your lead generation tools / Tactics. Contrary to popular belief you can make particularly good money from this type of advertising (thousands – even millions of Rands). The key however is to apply one proven 'principle' – the principle of 'Direct Response Advertising' (fully explained later).

Without applying this one basic principle your advertising will flop – no question (that's why people think advertising doesn't work!). However, when you apply the principle of 'Direct Response Advertising' your advertising will become a great success. That's the impact these little-known Business Building Principles will have on your business!

So, let's get started…

XBS Principle 1

Marketing Your Business Is the Ultimate Leverage

Too many marketers remained grounded in one- dimensional thinking habits. But marketing is a tool of the mind, and it's in the mind where true wealth is made. Before this starts to sound like some kind of New Age lecture, let me give you an example of what I mean.

Let's say you mail a sales letter to 50,000 people at an average cost of 50 pence each, for a total cost of R25,000 - That's a fixed cost. If you get a poor response and only manage to break even then there is a strong tendency for you to give up and say: "Why should I spend R25,000 and go through all that work, only to break even?"

If by scientifically changing and testing a few characteristics of the mailing piece you are able to multiply the response by five, fifteen, fifty or even five hundred times then you are using leverage.

The sales letter that broke even has the potential for almost infinite change. It's highly likely that something in the sales letter can be improved to increase response.

Often, simply using a stronger opening headline, or making a better offer in the body copy of the letter, a bonus, or trying a different price, can increase response by dramatically. By improving the content of the sales letter and doing it successfully, you employ the leveraging action of marketing. You're still sending a sales letter - but it's not about the physical tool. It's about the infinite possibilities impregnated in the marketing concept carried by that tool.

Other than available cash flow, there should be no such thing as a marketing budget. It is a ridiculous idea based on the assumption that marketing is a cost rather than a revenue generator.

If an ad costs R1,000 and the revenue generated from the ad is R1,200, why would you stop the ad just because your budget dictated it? With a scientific approach and providing the cash is available, the marketing budget is unlimited. It is self-generating.

Understanding this self-evident truth is the key to marketing leverage and massive business growth.

You can never truly run out of ideas. In marketing, persistence almost always pays off. Marketing can leverage a losing or a bland idea into something spectacular - if you have what it takes to make it happen!

XBS Principle 2

Multiple Channels of Distribution

A stool needs a minimum of three legs to stand on its own. Four would be nicer sometimes, but three will do.

However, less than three won't do. Loose a leg on a three- legged stool and it can no longer function properly at what is supposed to be - a solid base for a person to rest upon.

A well-known and respected marketer explains it by using the Parthenon in Athens as an analogy… Think of the roof as income or revenue, and the pillars as channels of distribution. If you only have one channel of distribution, then the roof is not only unstable but positively tottering. He calls this the 'diving board' philosophy.

Think about it, a few chips off the only pillar – your sole distribution method - could bring the whole lot down. Better to have multiple distribution channels – and therefore more pillars to hold the roof up – giving you more support, security and exponentially more revenue.

Your business may also be resting on shaky support if you are relying on just one or two marketing methods to keep things running in stable fashion. Too many businesses rely on print ads alone, for example. Even if they have print ads in multiple and diverse publications, the marketing effort is still one-dimensional. If, for some reason, the ads stop pulling, the business will crash and topple.

Another example is companies that rely solely on direct salespeople or representatives. If they fail to perform, or as often happens, defect and get bought off by a competitor, a business can face difficult times indeed.

But even if your business doing well with a single marketing vehicle, it only makes sense to establish more avenues of marketing income - why not add direct sales letters, prints ads, form joint ventures or implement a strategy to get free publicity using press releases and other promotional methods.

You could also start following up sales letter mailings with phone calls.

You're simply not letting your business be all it can be by limiting yourself to just one or two methods of bringing in new customers. Furthermore, you are exposing yourself to insecurity and danger.

Take a lesson from farmers - the smart ones diversify their operations. They plant a variety of crops and sometimes also maintain livestock. If the corn fails, the wheat may do okay and make up for lost revenue. If all the crops fail, sales of beef cattle may keep the operation afloat until the next growing season. Because it has a multiple of resources to fall back on, the farm need never fail, at least not for that reason.

When you develop multiple methods of marketing, you not only stand to make more money and more sales, but you inoculate your business against unforeseen failure.

This does not mean you must or even should start using two, three or four different selling channels right away. It's better to start with just one additional method, test it, and once you get it working and have worked the bugs worked out, then go on to yet another, and another, and another.

Yes, there probably is a point of diminishing returns in terms of how many kinds of marketing tools and Tactics you put into play. Becoming overwhelmed and too scattered is not a good thing either. But it just isn't a good idea not to have all your eggs in one basket.

However, when you create a multi-channel marketing effort, you put yourself on a firm foundation for greater success, security and gain some insurance against potential loss to boot.

XBS Principle 3

Positioning

Positioning is a pivotal marketing concept that actually encompasses many aspects of marketing today. But the word itself generally refers to your position "relative to" or "against" your competitors. That's because, these days, you're likely to have a lot of competitors no matter what kind of business you're in.

Just open up the Yellow Pages. How many dentists are listed in your town? How many plumbers? How many insurance brokers? The list is long in most categories.

The dilemma that immediately confronts the thinking business owner is: "Why should anyone select me, rather than the other guy? We all have about the same level and quality of service, we all have prices within the same basic range, and we're all equally accessible, and so on."

What is the answer to this dilemma? Many people might jump in and say: "Prospects tend to choose the one with the lowest price."

But this is simply not true. Study after study shows that price is seldom the primary factor in making a decision to choose one dealer over another. If it were so, no luxury, premium or high-quality goods would ever be sold.

The fact is, many factors enter into why people choose one business over another, and often the choice is merely random. Not everyone is a discriminating shopper who weighs every factor before choosing a product or service.

This is where positioning comes in. If you want customers to choose you, then you need to position yourself against the competition in a way that makes you stand out, and which gives good reason for people to choose you.

One of the best ways to do that is to foster an image of yourself as being "an expert in your field." In other words, you want people to think: "Sure there's a lot of good dentists in this town, but Mr. Bill Johnson is a dentist's dentist - he's an expert, he knows more about the science of dentistry than the average dentist."

How would people obtain that view of Bill Johnson? Well, what if he published a book of tips on dental care, and how to anyone can maintain healthy teeth and also reduce their dental care bills by 30%?

What if Bill Johnson also conducted free seminars in dental care, or offered his services to local schools to come in and talk to young students about proper daily dental care? And what if he also used those opportunities to promote his book? And since Bill Johnson has published a book on dental care, it's likely a local radio station and newspaper will grant him an interview to talk about his book, and why he wrote it.

He may also get invited onto TV and radio programming when basic health topics are discussed - reporters usually invite the guy who's an expert, and the guy who "wrote the book" book is mostly likely to be that man.

Positioning yourself as an expert means doing something that makes you stand out as an expert. That can be:

Writing a book.

Publishing a regular newspaper column on your area of expertise.

Giving seminars.

Getting yourself listed in key directories, such as "Who's Who."

Getting yourself invited on TV and radio talk shows.

Getting to know editors and reporters and telling them they can call you when they need information involving a story that involves your expertise. They'll then quote you and get your name into news stories, which is among the very best kind of free publicity you can get.

Establishing a "hot line" to answer questions in your field of expertise.

Issue press releases related to the latest development in your field, and list yourself as a resource for further information.

You don't have to be a dentist or a professional. A car mechanic, a plumber, a builder - anyone can do all of the above and establish themselves as the "go to guy" when it comes to questions or information in any particular field.

Don't think you can write a book, or don't have time?
Hire a ghost-writer to write it for you - it's a time- honored tradition used by thousands of people all the time. The bottom line is, in today's strenuously competitive marketplace, becoming viewed as the "expert in your field" can be the ultimate positioning tool. Better yet once you establish your position as "expert" you may never have to compete on price again. Many people will be glad to pay premium prices for "the best."

Finally, your positioning activities can actually earn you money while you promote and bolster your image.

Sales of your book can mean a tidy sideline income, and you can charge admission for seminars. When you are interviewed by local media representatives, it's like getting top-notch advertising for free.

The benefits of positioning are many. I urge you to start considering and planning to put your positioning strategy into play right now!

XBS Principle 4

Your USP

Get out the Yellow Pages and look up a common business - a plumber, insurance agent, car dealer. You'll find a lot of ads for each, some big, some tiny. Or look around your town. You probably have a number of dentists, hardware stores, clothing stores, hairdressers.

Now think about a person who needs one of the above. They have a lot of choices about to whom they'll give their business. Why should they choose one over the other? What makes one different or sets them apart from the others?

You might say price - many people shop based on price, and thus will go with who will provide the service or sell the product for the least cost. Everyone is always looking for the cheapest price, right?

Wrong! It's true that price is a major factor in buying decisions, but study after study shows that it's almost never the "top" reason people select one business over another.

If price was the motivating factor in everything there would not be a market for Mercedes, Waitrose, Coutts, Rolex and every other premium, luxury or high-quality product or service. Also, most plumbers, electricians, and dentists, to name a few, have more or less the same price anyway. So, we get back to our central question: Why should they buy from you and not a competitor?

The answer is simple: People will more often opt for the seller who stands out from the rest, and who is offering something unique and different. That's why you need what is known as a "USP" - Unique Selling proposition.

A USP is simply an articulation of the thing about your product, service or company that almost compels prospects and customers to buy from you and not your competitors.

Some famous examples of USP's include Domino's Pizza, which was perhaps the first to guarantee free delivery of pizza in 30 minutes or less, or you don't pay. Their USP tagline was: 'Hot pizza delivered within 30 minutes or it's free'. Now, many all pizza shops do this, but the one that did it first captured a huge share of the market while all the others struggled to play catch-up.

Another example from the United States: Oreck Vacuum Cleaners. This company offers to let you use their vacuum cleaner weighing just 8 kilograms in your home for 30 days free, and you can return it with no further obligation if you don't like it. But they sweeten the deal even more - they also give you a free portable "shop vac" which you get to keep no matter what - just for trying their main product! That's a generous offer, it's unique, and other vacuum dealers have been hard pressed to counter it.

Yet another example: Gevalia coffee offers you a free coffee maker for trying their gourmet coffee, which they send to you by mail. If you like the coffee, they just keep sending it once a month, or so, and they bill you. If you opt out of this home coffee delivery service, you keep the coffee maker - free. Merely the fact that they ship the coffee right to your home is a quite a USP for coffee in itself - most people have to go to the store to buy it. But they make their USP even stronger with the offer of a freebie. It's terrific!

You may already have a USP right now, and not know it. Take a look at your product or service. How is better or different from a competitor? Maybe you can easily prove you sell higher quality for the same price as a competitor, or credit terms make it much easier to buy.
Whatever the case, do something that no one else is doing, and even more important - make sure your market audience clearly can recognize it!

Look at your Yellow Pages ad. Are you just another "me too" listing, or does something uniquely different jump out of that ad and grab shoppers to decide: "Hey? I'm going to call this guy!"

Here's a few pointers when thinking about constructing your U.S.P. Do you have: Bigger discounts or lower cost. A broader selection.

Easier or more convenient (location, speed, service, accuracy).

Expert advice or 'Rolls Royce' service. More comprehensive products or services.

Better guarantees or warrantees. Speedier
or cheaper deliveries.

Or anything else that you can think of.

Remember, a USP is all about perception. It's not enough to have a USP - your target market must easily and quickly see that you stand out. Do this, and you're going to burn your competition, and make shoppers try you first!

XBS Principle 5

Lifetime Customer Value

Far too many business owners are locked into a short-term view. It's a natural tendency to think something like: "I place an ad that costs R1,000. That ad brings in 230 responses, and of those, 21 turn into actual sales. At R90 per sale, I have a gross income of R1,890.
When I subtract the cost of the ad, I end up with R890. Next, I subtract my other expenses associated with producing or buying my product wholesale, fulfilment, salaries and other factors, and I end up with about R230 in net profit."

Results like these can seem discouraging. After all that money spent and effort, you end up with a tiny R230. To get another R230, you have to do it all over again -- buy another R1,000 ad, and all the rest. This is where a lot of businesspeople drop out and try something else that seems more profitable.

But wait -- this view of things is too short sighted.
The initial ad brought in 21 new, paying customers. What if that same businessperson had read my earlier item on back-end marketing and had a second and third product ready to sell after each of those 21-customer paid R90 for the first? What if his second-tier product sold for R65 and 13 of the 21 also bought it in addition to the first product? That's an additional R845, which you add to the first R230 for R1,075! Suddenly things are looking a lot more profitable - but this is still not the end.

If the seller does what he must to keep the customer satisfied and coming back for the next three to five years, each of those customers may end up spending another R400 or R500. If each of those original 21 customers is converted into a long-term customer spending R500 each, that's R10,500! Now, we're talking.

It's reasonable and perhaps even conservative to expect another R500 in sales over the next five years from each customer you capture with your initial ad, for which you paid R1,000 - which had actually generated more than 10 times that cost - R10,500.

Furthermore, each of those initial customers will often refer a friend, (or you can be even more proactive by asking for a referral) and sometimes more than one friend

to also make a purchase. You pay nothing for a word-of- mouth referral - and the result is even more profit that can be tied to your original ad expenditure.

So, what you should do is calculate the lifetime value of each customer. Doing so helps you realize that you can spend a lot more on ads and other marketing tools to go out and get them simply because the long-term payoff is literally... fantastic. When you know that the lifetime value of each customer may be R500 to R900 each, for example, then a R1,000 ad that gets you 21 of them is a real bargain. Another benefit of knowing the lifetime value of your customers is that because you know that a R1,000 ad – as per the above example - will generate R10,500, it provides you with the ability to plan and estimate your future cash flow with a degree of certainty.

Furthermore, should you ever want to sell the business, demonstrating this knowledge could have a tremendous impact on the capital value and therefore the sale price.

All of this requires a long-term view and planning, however, to happen. You have to be prepared with back- end products to sell, you have to sell quality and make the customer want to come back, you have to develop a healthy relationship with your customers, and more. But when you plan and take a long-term point of view, you set yourself up for long-term success.

You also gain the confidence of spending what you need to spend to get new customers, knowing that it will pay off.

XBS Principle 6

The Irresistible Customer Relationship Model

Peoples needs and wants change constantly... Almost minute by minute and therefore what they say 'no' to today could be 'yes' next month, next week, tomorrow or even in a minute.

Marketing research lets you know what people want, who they are, what they need, and so on, it can provide a baseline. But there are subtleties to interpreting marketing research you should be aware of. For one thing, marketing research gives you a "snapshot" of where people are at the moment.

No one ever stays frozen in one place. That means their needs and situations constantly change - sometimes just 15 minutes after they described their needs to a marketing research or telemarketers' query!

If someone doesn't need your product or service today, that doesn't mean they won't need it tomorrow, or next week. Or maybe they need it but can't buy until two weeks from now when they get their next paycheck.
Often, all this means is that the time is not exactly right for them to buy.

Experienced and smart marketers know that taking just one shot – a single letter, ad, phone call, face to face contact - at a prospect is rarely sufficient. Smart marketers know that people buy more often on the second, third, fourth or fifth time you contact them.

It's called 'the irresistible customer relationship model'. It is well documented that the persistent salesperson that doesn't give up on the first 'no' can often move on to get the sale. Furthermore, experience shows that people will often respond after they've received 6, 7 or more contacts.

The point is, by sequentially and systematically making the extra efforts you can very often get a payoff where many before you have failed. That's where the 'irresistible customer relationship model' comes in.

When a prospect says 'No', they often don't mean 'No' in the sense that they don't want to take you up on your offer. It may mean that they don't "Know" enough to make an informed decision. So, you have to give them more information, more value. Add more benefit, more advantage, more use, enhancement, lifestyle, profit... whatever is their hot button, so the eventual outcome is that the value you've presented far and away exceeds any price or other reason they may have for saying "No" or not going ahead with your proposition.

Let me give you an example: An acquaintance, Mike, is an expert at helping people get private foundation or government grants for a variety of projects. Because Mike frequently got more calls from prospects than he could deal with personally, he decided to write a booklet on grant writing which told people how they could get a grant on their own, and without the help of a professional.

Mike put together a nifty sales letter which extolled the virtues of his booklet and sent it to the dozens of people who called him each week. Even though the people calling him were obviously interested in grant writing information, Mike almost never got a sale of his booklet after sending his sales letter. He was selling the information for a reasonable R11.95. Mike asked me to take a look at his sales letter to see if anything was wrong with it - but I found it to be excellent. I told Mike:

"Don't change a thing. Keep sending the same sales letter. If you don't get a response, send a second mailing in 10 days - this time just a post card advertising the same report, but with a $2 discount, and have a time limit of 7-days to get the report at the cheaper price."

Mike did so, and suddenly began to sell almost 6 out of 10 people who got the postcard after the initial sales letter.

Why did it work? Many times, people are almost ready to buy, but decide to pass for a variety of reasons. Again, maybe it wasn't pay day, or maybe they just wanted time to think it over. Whatever the case, things change, situations change, needs change - everything changes constantly. The bottom line for those of us who want to sell is:

The other profitable idea to remember is that your current customers need to be regularly communicated with too. If they've bought once, they'll probably buy again
— maybe a bigger, better, or more expensive one, or perhaps some additional products and services.

Use the 'irresistible customer relationship model' in all your marketing - it pays to make more than one approach and one attempt to sell. The 'irresistible customer relationship model' is simply an organized combination of mailing, faxing and phone calls to make an offer (sell a product or service) to a prospect. It is an offer that is repeated over and over again with variations that relate and build upon the previous mailing piece or contact.

Such sequential mailings and contacts will outperform single one-off mailings or calls by astronomical and exponential amounts. This is also because the target is exposed to the offer again and again and tells the prospect that you mean business and are concerned that he/she has the opportunity to take advantage of the offer you're presenting to them.

With high value products and services, mailings are reinforced and supplemented by a number of combinations of faxes, phone calls, post cards and/or personal sales visits. Experience proves that the best results are gained by the use of such multiple approaches.

Vary your pitch, your method, your media, or your price and keep plugging away.

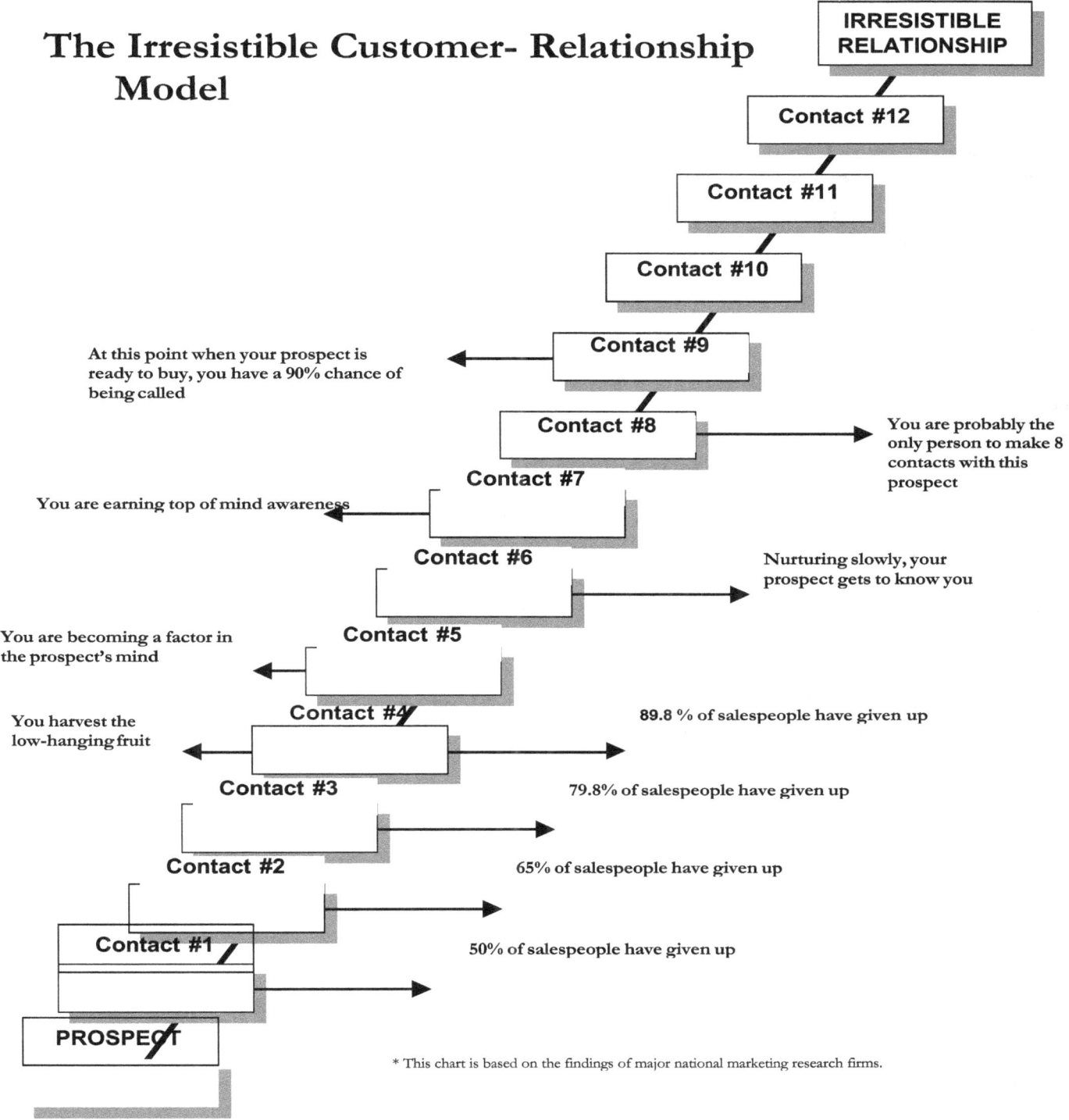

XBS Principle 7

Defeating The 'Clutter Factor' – SAVi's

One of the biggest problems faced by businesses doing any type of marketing in today's business environment is what is called 'The Clutter Factor'.

It is estimated that the average person receives some 2,000 commercial messages each and every day. The average businessperson probably receives around 3,000 per day. This includes messages from many different media sources including, letters, emails, branding, bumper stickers, newspaper and magazine ads, radio, and television, and of course the telephone.

Think about it, this means that your unsolicited mailing piece is just one of many that land on someone's desk or door mat. It then competes with all the other 'junk' mail. It may not get opened and if it does then it may be by the gatekeeper (secretary, receptionist, assistant… worse it may not get read and is almost certainly thrown out… Your message is part of someone's clutter!

Therefore, to defeat this, to avoid being trashed, ignored, or disparaged, your message has to stand out. It must rise above all the rest of the messages your prospects receive, regardless of the media source. And in order to do this it must be better, more noticeable and superior in the attention it generates, the interest it creates and the offer it makes. You must use AICDA - but turbocharged!

Your ad must literally jump out and grab the reader's or listener's attention! It has to get past the gatekeeper and into the hands of the intended buyer. To do this it must be what we term a 'Superior Access Vehicle' or 'SAVi'… it drives right through the clutter and gets to the intended party.

Remember AICDA. By using SAVi solutions you grab Attention.

One of the best and most powerful ways to create a SAVi is to use 'Attention Grabbers'. These are simple but unusual items that give your mailing piece a literal three-dimensional look and feel ('lumpy mail') and are usually attached to the top of the letter.

These can then be cleverly tied into your opening headline and paragraph in such a way as to draw the prospect in – gaining Interest.

Because your letter is now so unusual and different from the rest of the letters your prospect receives, they are more likely to be read, remembered, and acted upon.

Here's a list of proven and effective SAVi Attention Grabbers with sample tie-in headlines that can be used for your Quantum mailings:

Grabber	Headline
Aspirin Packet	Name, here is one way to solve your biggest headache… another way is to give me a call.
Fake Million Dollar Note	Name, as one of our preferred customers, you're worth a million to me!
	Name, the attached bill is just a sample of the kind of money we can make together…
	Name, check out this million-dollar idea!
Plastic Banana	Name, if your monthly expenses are driving you bananas… we need to talk!
	Name, if the money you're spending on advertising compared to the results you're getting is driving you bananas…
Bag of Nuts	Name, if your employees are driving you nuts…
	Name, don't let your underperforming salespeople drive you nuts…
Sheet of Wallpaper with Little Car Glued to It	Name, if your competitors are driving you up the wall…
Plastic Dog Bone	Name, please be careful. Secret sources revealed someone is having a bone to pick with you… soon!
Necktie	Name, do your complacent employees ever make you think of having a 'necktie party'?
Foam Brick	Name, are your poor advertising results making you feel like you're banging your head against a brick wall?
Plastic Shovel	Name, this is my last-ditch effort to contact you…
	Name, ever feel like the harder you

	work, the deeper you get?
Broken Straw	Name, when is this going to how you feel about your underperforming ads (salespeople, employees)?
Rubber Hen	Name, are supply costs making you as mad as a wet hen?
Toy Boat	Name, this is your last chance to catch the boat!
Bag of Grass	Name, are you going to let the grass grow under your feet again?
Tennis Ball	Name, the ball is in your court!
Plastic Ear	Listen to this, Name… It's an offer you'd be a fool to pass up!
Stones	Name, you can't afford to leave any stones unturned when it comes to our marketing your competition!
Bag of Sand	Name, now that the economy is down is not the time to bury your head in the sand… Here's an offer you can't pass up!
Chess piece	Name, marketing can be a complicated strategy, do you know the right moves to guarantee your success?
Scratch-It Lottery Ticket	Name, there are two ways to increase your wealth – here's one way… Improving the way you market is the other!
Eraser	Name, imagine if you could quickly and easily erase your competition from the minds of your customers and prospects almost overnight!
Watch	Name, don't let this timely opportunity go by!
Tea Bag	Name, sit back and have a nice cup of tea on me.
Large Matchstick	Name, this idea is so hot… I've got to get it off my chest before I explode!
Lunch Bag	Name, who says there's no such thing as a free lunch!
Doll's Shoe or A Real Shoe	Name, I just had to find a way to get my foot in your door!
Right Shoe	Name, let's begin on the right foot!
Pair of Shoes	Name, this idea will sweep you off your feet!
Socks	Name, this idea will knock your socks off!

Breath Mints	Name, this idea will take your breath away!
Hat	Name, here's something I just couldn't keep under my hat!
Cards	Name, with these cards you only have four chances to draw an ace. With our marketing Tactics you'll come up a winner every time!
Canoe Paddle	Name, don't find yourself up the marketing creek without one of these!
Mock Check (cheque)	Name, the above check is not redeemable at any bank – but it could be the most valuable bonus you will ever receive!
Band-Aid	Name, Band-Aid's are only meant to be temporary fixes. Let me show you how to permanently solve your marketing frustrations!
Coin	Name… Confused about your (marketing, hiring, employee evaluation, etc.) problems? You can either flip a coin or take your chances… Or you can let us help you with proven and tested solutions!

XBS Principle 8

Joint Ventures & Host Beneficiary Alliances

They go by many names - joint ventures, fusion marketing, strategic alliances, cross promoting, host beneficiary - but they all involve some form of the same thing - one company getting together with another, or several others, to help each other find more customers, make more sales and make more money. Everybody benefits.

What if you could almost instantly find the names and addresses of, say 10,000 or even 100,000 all-new prospects that are guaranteed to have strong interest in what you are selling, and then send each one of them your best sales letter - and none of this would cost you a cent?

Well, it's not only possible, but it's something many have done dozens of times, and the payoff can be simply phenomenal!

You accomplish it with what is called a "host- beneficiary relationship," and nothing could be easier. Here is how to get it done:

Contact another business in a complementary market – one that deals with similar customers and does not compete with yours and ask them to let you mail your sales materials to their customer list.

You can either include your materials - endorsed by the host - onto something the host company is already mailing anyway, or have your materials be the primary mail piece.

Why should the host company agree to do this for you? Because you will offer them 50% of all profits you make from the mailing. If that seems like a lot, remember you're not only getting the mailing done for free, but you're finding a rich market of highly qualified prospects with a strong chance of wanting to buy from you.

The host company makes a pile of money they would not have made otherwise - and you make a lot of sales, make a profit, and best of all, find a lot of new customers. You can sell to again and again in the future. It's a classic win-win situation.

Because such host beneficiary relationships are so profitable, you can afford to be generous in making your proposition to a potential host. If your prospective host needs more convincing, offer them a sweeter deal -- say 60% to them and 40% for yourself. You still make a profit. Even if you have to give them 100% of the profits the first time, and the next mailing is 50-50, it's still a tremendous deal, especially if you do several more mailings.

> **Example 1:**
>
> A car insurance broker teamed up with a number of used car dealers. He had each of them send their client list a letter on the car dealer's own stationary, recommending they call him for a great deal on car insurance.
>
> The insurance broker composed the letter, which the car dealer put in their stationary and signed their own names on. In this case, the insurance man even offered to pay for the mailings, in addition to half the net profits of each new sale to the hosts. In one month, the insurance broker garnered nearly 400 new clients.
>
> Even though half the profits went to the hosts, all future business - including policy renewals - was all his to keep.

No matter what your business, there are almost certainly dozens of opportunities right now for you to team up with another business to conduct joint mailings. Let's look at just a couple of examples:

It's important to keep in mind the long-term view with host-beneficiary relationships. Even if you have to offer very generous terms initially to your hosts, captured customers often become repeat customers (Lifetime Value of a Customer) that can keep generating sales and profits for years to come.

> **Example 2:**
>
> The owner of a complementary health business was approached by a health food store. Again, using the host's stationary, clients were recommended to visit the health food store -- and if they brought the letter in with them - they got a free bottle of vitamin C with their purchase of R20 or more.
>
> The response was simply terrific - a flood of new traffic into the store. The match was a good one - people who seek complementary therapy are highly likely to be health conscious and will be interested in the wares of a health food store.
>
> Notice in this example, the health food store strengthened the offer by including the element of getting something free - providing a reward and incentive for complementary health clients to come in.

The basic content of a host-beneficiary relationship is strong enough on its own, but with some thought and planning, you can make it even more powerful by working in added incentives, such as including discount coupons, offers for free items, and more. Also, remember this: finding new clients on your own is an expensive proposition. You must advertise, buy mailing lists, pay for mailings and more, and even then, you may get cool response.

When you tap into another company's captured customer list, you instantly gain the benefit of the thousands, perhaps even hundreds of thousands of Rands they have spent over the years to build up that list.

The stronger and closer the relationship that the host company has with its customers the higher the response and success rate. All you pay is the share of your profits that go to your host while making a profit yourself.

I urge you to try this idea right now. A host beneficiary relationship is one of the best ways I know to get a lot of new business - and cash flow - fast!

Here's yet another example of a kind of host alliance - a simple concept with powerful results. An endorsed mailing is just this: You make a request or agreement from another respected, established business to write a letter that recommends you to their customers.

There are many reasons this kind of direct marketing sales letter works so well.

First, it doesn't seem like sales letter, but that's exactly what it is! The best direct marketing sales letters are those that don't look or feel like junk mail, or a blatant attempt to sell something.

The endorsement letter is like getting a letter from a friend telling you about another friend you should get to know, and whom you can trust. Second, it taps into a ready-made source of customer leads already squeezed out of the market by an established business. Third, it doesn't have to cost you very much money.

You can simply agree to return the favor to your host, or you can agree to give a commission to your host for all sales that result. The latter costs you a bit more, but it's still a terrific deal.

Endorsed mailing can be done by any number of businesses - they should be non-competing or course, and the more complementary the better, Professionals tend to do well endorsing other professionals, such as a Lawyer endorsing an accountant or financial adviser, but it doesn't have to be limited in that fashion.

Here's a random example:

A jeweler writes an endorsement letter for a seller of women's Jewelry. It might read something like this:

Dear Customer:
You look great when you wear one of our diamond or gold necklaces, earrings, or the fine piece of jewellery of your choice. Now, if you want to complete your look and be at your very best, I cannot think of anyone better to recommend for the absolute best in style than our friends at Johnson Fashions for Women.
My friend Carol Johnson is the boutique manager at their new store at 123 High St.
Anytown, and I happen to know she is the best in fitting and matching you with the exact apparel you will need to look your best. Whether you are getting ready for that important job interview, preparing for an important formaloccasion, or whenever you need to be in top form.

Johnson Fashion has an impressive collection - I go there myself all the time, and I know you'll like when you find if you pay them a visit.
Thanks for being a loyal customer. When you wear the best in jewelry and the latest fashions, you'll have the confidence and ultimate look to greet the world looking and feeling your best.
Yours Sincerely

        Anne Wilson Manager
        Wilson's Jewelry

    P.S. Tell Carol we sent you and get an extra 15% off on your first purchase!

It's as simple as that. Note that you can and should write the letter yourself and then have your host sign it on its stationary. This saves your host endorser time and makes things easier for them.

There are many other ways different companies can get together in a mutually beneficial relationship the permutations are almost unlimited. Even if you're an independent salesperson, you can join forces with other individuals or other companies to aid each other in your quest for greater business success.

We've already touched on some of these - the electrician and the insurance man who get together to find each other leads for each other's business and give commissions to each other.

The company that piggybacks its direct marketing materials on another company's mailings. The car sellers who decide to share with each other's leads from their "can't sell" files to see if the other has better luck.

Here's a classic example of joint venture excellence at work:

A maker of energy-saving fluorescent light was forced to rely on his small direct sales force to convince dealers and retailers to carry his light fixtures and sell them to industrial customers. He couldn't afford consumer advertising based on his sales and he had no retail outlets of his own to sell his lights directly to the end user.
Building his own retail stores was far beyond his means.

After seven years of slow growth - enough to get by and make a fair profit - the light maker formed a joint venture plan with an electric utility company. The utility company agreed to stuff the light maker's ads in their monthly electric bills to customers.

The utility company readily agreed because the fluorescent lights burned with far lower power usage - and if enough customers started using them, the utility company could avoid spending millions on building new generators to keep up with growing demand for power.

The light maker included coupons and vouchers for his lights. After the utility company mailed them with their billing statements, all the light maker had to do was fulfil orders returned by energy customers.

The result: Sales poured in.

Before the joint venture, this light manufacturer of energy efficient bulbs was selling R3 million a year - but after the joint venture deal was launched, sales soured to R8 million a year. Buoyed by this success, the light company forged more than three dozen similar joint marketing ventures, and at last count, was doing R15 million per year.

Here's another example:

A marketing consultant co-ordinate home-buying seminar. As speakers, he invites an insurance broker, a mortgage broker, and an estate agent. Many people come to hear the estate agent, but while there, the insurance broker gets to talk about what he can do for those buying homes.

The mortgage broker also gets to talk about how he can provide funding to buy homes. All together, these separate professionals cover all the bases for potential buyers of new homes, and they all pick up clients.

To the seminar attendees, the three professionals look like a team - but they're all independent guys who are simply taking advantage of the natural synergy their expertise entails. Oh yeah, and the marketing consultant gets his seminars filled because he is providing such a broad range of useful information.

Again, joint ventures can be many things, and the subject could easily fill an entire book by itself:

- Trade mailing lists with other non-competing businesses.

- Do endorsed mailings.

- Insert a plug for your product in another company's ads (like Coca Cola does with McDonald's).

- Share demographic data with complimentary businesses.

- Do joint mailings.

- Share mutually beneficial technical and research data.

The list could go on and on, some of which have already been mentioned and others we'll discuss in forthcoming pages. There is no set formula and no rules in joint venturing. The important factor is to find joint venture partners who can supply elements that you lack... Be it expertise, finance, time, effort, prospect or mailing lists, whatever.

The point is, joint ventures are not only easy, but an exciting and effective method to boost your business into new markets and profit levels.

XBS Principle 9

Conversion and Closing Devices

Using tools - check lists, registration forms, order forms, telephone prompters and the like can be made into extremely powerful devices to assist in converting an enquiry into a sale and a sale into a bigger sale.

A telephone prompter for businesses that have the ability to sell from incoming calls is a very powerful method to convert enquiries to sales. All you have to do is follow the script.

The impact of this simple methodology is nothing short of amazing. One client of mine reported that their conversion of telephone calls to sales went from 2 sales out of 10 enquiries to a staggering 8 sales out of 10! That was just from following a telephone prompter.

Businesses that operate in a highly competitive environment will benefit enormously from this strategy because you can literally capture the price-oriented enquirer and turn them into a sales closing call or sell them right there on the phone.

Your business must operate on with the philosophy that every incoming call into your business has value... Every customer contact is an opportunity.

When adapting the prompter for your use remember this valuable secret to selling more... Never, ever, reveal the price or details of your product or service without telling them precisely what your product or service will do for them and why you are the only solution.

Additionally, with a prompter you can record their responses and use their very statements in your quote or proposal to them — you can write in the things about your product or service that they have stated are important to them.

Here's an example…
Let's say you're in the double-glazing business and you have a question in your form that asks if they want a 20-year guarantee or special security glass then you would put into the quote or proposal something like:

> "Your new XYZ Co. windows are manufactured with special unbreakable glass that provides you with security and peace of mind". And "Your XYZ Co. windows come with an unprecedented 20-year guarantee that means…"

Prompters should also be used by salespeople or field staff. The prompter can take the guise of an order form or signing off docket or registration form.

On this you list the searching questions designed to uncover needs or wants and then ask the prospect or customer if they would like to buy a product or service that meets this requirement.

For instance, a garden maintenance business that has gangs of gardeners working on people's property each day can have a 'job completion' form. This form could also have a list of other services or products offered by the garden maintenance company... such as security fencing, ground levelling, clearance, tree surgery, etc. Against each of these is a tick box. The gang leader has to run though each of these before getting the completed work signed off at the bottom. Obviously, offering an incentive to the gang leader will go a long way in increasing a positive response.

Simple but very profitable.

Just adapt the questions to your business, put it into action and watch your sales climb.

Qualifying Questionnaire & Phone Script for In-Coming Calls.

For Private Coach Hire

Good morning/afternoon, XYZ Coaches & Tours, This is .... How may I help you?

May I take your name please? _____

And your phone numbers? (Work)_____ (After Hours)_____

May I ask how you heard about us?_____

Where do you wish to travel to? _____

How many people will be travelling in your party?_____

When were you thinking of going?_____ At what time?_____

How long are you staying?_____ What time will you need to be picked up? _____

Are there any pickups en-route? _____

Right that sounds fine, we could take care of you and your party on that day/weekend. I must mention that whilst we are not the most expensive company, we are not the cheapest either. That is because all our coaches are immaculately clean and are fitted with climate control, snug seating, and full toilet & washroom amenities so that you're comfortable and relaxed for the whole journey. Furthermore, we serve complimentary hot and soft drinks to keep you refreshed along the way. A home pick up service can also be made available for a little extra to save you the effort of getting to the couch station. Does that sound like the kind of service that you and your party would enjoy?

I thought so. Now, our Standard Couch service would cost just R .... per person return.

Or you could upgrade to our business class Executive Couches which would only be an extra R........................ per person r return. For that little extra you get lots more legroom, video entertainment, as well as a delicious snack.
Which sounds best to you? Great. May I take your booking now to avoid disappointment?
(IF AVAILABLE ON THE DAY OR IF NO FIRM BOOKING GIVEN):
Just a bit of news for you… We recently acquired the luxurious England Football Team Coach; this is true first-class travel and was used by them for touring right up until 6 months ago. To promote our proud ownership, we are offering a special discount of 20% off the normal rate but as you will appreciate it's booking very fast. Just glancing at the calendar, I have that date available just at the moment and after the discount it would cost just R… ....
per person return. Would you be interested
in booking it now to avoid disappointment.

Your address:_____

Thank you, Mr/Mrs/Ms .... we will send out a confirmation letter to you within the next few days

XBS Principle 10

Direct Response Advertising

One of the most common, expensive, and painful mistakes people make in their advertising efforts is the use of what is known as "institutional advertising" or "image advertising". What is that? Well, it's probably the majority of all advertising you see every day. Institutional advertising is most often used by the big players - McDonald's, Ford, Nike and all the rest. Institutional advertising does not necessarily sell anything directly.
Rather, it promotes the company as a whole. Institutional advertising is all about name recognition and company image. It beats a constant drum which keeps the name of the company in front of as many people as possible, as often as possible.

What's wrong with this? Nothing for the mega-rich corporations that can afford it, who want to satisfy their egos or show their shareholders how good they are, but for a small, savvy lean marketer, it's a fantastic waste of money.

What you need to do with your advertising is make sales, not necessarily build an image. That means advertising your specific product or service, and not your company. It means telling your audience exactly how they will benefit from buying your specific product right now, where they can get it, and how they can take immediate action to get it.

The fact is that people don't care about you or your company - don't take that personal, that's the way it should be. What prospects care about are their own needs and wants, and you should appeal directly to that. Tell them about your product and how it can make their lives better today. Educate them about why they should buy it, why they need it, and why it's a great deal for the money.

Forget about all this: "I'm here!", "Me too!" advertising. Don't waste time bragging about yourself and your company. Put the focus on the buyer - his and her most vital needs right now - then offer them something that scratches their itch, fulfils their need, or solves their problem.

Most beginning entrepreneurs - and also many experienced ones - fall into the trap of going with institutional advertising simply because they see everyone else doing it all the time, and everywhere. They assume it must be working. If you're a giant corporation with an astronomical advertising budget, great.

But if you're a lean and hungry small business - or even a moderately sized or large business - use direct marketing, appeal directly the client's interests needs and wants. Sell a specific product with specific details and benefits.

I could go on further about this important topic, but I want you to get the fundamental concept here - sell a specific product tied to specific needs and problems, and you'll someday be big and rich enough to buy the kind of institutional advertising that makes you just that - a veritable institution… That is if you want to waste your money!

XBS Principle 11

Upselling

Here is a selling technique that is remarkably similar to back-ending. A back-end sale is when you sell a second product after the first. Upselling involves selling enhancements or additions to the original product you have just sold.

Anyone who has purchased a new car has experienced the upsell – car dealers use this technique very aggressively and successfully.

After you agree to buy the car, the representative takes you down a list of options you can agree to add to your new car right now at the point of purchase: antirust coating, mud flaps, larger engine, automatic transmission, the bigger better stereo, a GPS navigation system - the list can be long. Just about everybody agrees to at least some of the additional options, and the bottom line is, the car dealer can make several hundred to several thousand Rands in extra profit without having to capture an all-new customer and sell a whole new car!

There is no reason why you should not engineer upselling into your sales as too. By reviewing your closing Tactics, you could increase your average sale by 15%, 25% or even 40%! Just by asking a simple question or utilising an easy process.

Sellers of home electronics equipment have recently discovered the magic of the "extended warranty." When you buy a new TV, stereo, or computer, it most likely already has a one to three-year warranty against product defects. But for an additional R25 to R150, the warranty can be extended another year or so. Studies show that only 12% of customer who opt for the extended warranty actually end up using it.

That means 88% of all those extended warranty sales are pure profit for the seller - money they would not have had if they hadn't simply made the offer.

Upselling can be as simple as asking a restaurant patron if they would like desert after their meal (McDonalds ask 'Would you like to go large?'), or asking a cinema goer if they would like to add a box of chocolate drops to their purchase of popcorn. The upsell takes only the few seconds of time it takes to ask the customer who has already bought to simply buy a little more right now. It's an almost effortless and inoffensive way to dramatically increase your profits.

No matter what you sell, you can almost certainly upsell it with some kind of ready-to-go enhancement or add-on - not doing it is a lost opportunity to make a whole lot more money effortlessly, quickly and easily.

XBS Principle 12

Tell Them Why

Here's a light bulb that looks rather funny, although it screws into any socket the same way any other household light bulb does, and it lights a room as well as the normal bulbs. But this new, funny looking light bulb costs R10 per unit, and you can get the normal ones at three for R1.29. So why should anyone buy the funny looking light bulb for R10?

Well, the funny looking light bulb is a new energy efficient design that burns more 858% less energy than does the ordinary bulb does and easily lasts five years or more. Over the lifetime of the new kind of bulb, you save more than R258 in electricity cost, and you do not have to replace the bulb 25 times as you do with the cheap, normal ones.

To get a customer to pay R10 for a light bulb when they are accustomed to paying a Rand, they really need to know why. If your explanation is good enough, as in the above example, they will buy your item more often.

Often if your price is extremely low, the result can be fewer sales because even though people love bargains, they may be suspicious. They think: "If it's that cheap, there must be something wrong with it."

But if you tell them: "We need to reduce our inventory now because we don't have enough room in our warehouse for the new stuff that is coming in," that can be a logical explanation that sits well with the prospective customer and therefore be viewed as a good opportunity and a bargain.

Your "Why" factor can pertain to the quality of your product, why it takes so long to deliver it, or why it is clearly better than your competition's product. I encourage you to take a close look at whatever you sell, then put yourself in the position of the buyer, and ask, "Why that price?" "Why is it so small?" "Why should I buy now and not later?" "Why is it worth waiting for?"

Many businesses offer highly publicized discounts…. 40% off all fitted kitchens. All stock must go 20% off, etc – Without giving a reason why you are making such great offers, this strategy can be not only ineffective and counterproductive but also very damaging to profitability.

The fact is that many buyers today are highly suspicious, skeptical, and outright cynical about such offers, to the extent that they view them as a ploy, a con or just totally ignore them.

Giving the buyer a reason why you are making such a great offer justifies and adds believability.

The better you educate your customers and pre-emptively clear away any nagging "whys?" that can easily be lingering in their hearts and minds, the fewer obstacles there will be for the customer to make a decision to buy now. Doing so will make the offer more convincing and the prospect is therefore more likely to buy.

You can often get a clue to what the most important "Why?" questions are by listening to your customers when they come in to look at your product and ask questions about it. If you notice a common theme or pattern, why not go ahead, and answer those questions in your ads and sales letters. The customer may more often come in pre-sold because they already know what they need to know to make a buying decision.

XBS Principle 13

Features & Benefits

The issue of handling features and benefits in marketing messages is critical to successful selling. This is an area where perhaps many sellers, even experienced sellers, are most likely to make a fatal blunder. Part of the problem usually involves confusing features with benefits. A feature and a benefit can be one and the same thing, but most often, they are not. It is a mistake for a seller to assume that some wonderful aspect or feature of his or her product will do the selling… Often it will not.

Before we say more, let us clarify the difference between a feature and a benefit. A feature is most often some physical aspect of a product -- its colour, the size of its engine, how much power it has, the quality of the material it is made of, and so on. Most often, a feature is "a thing."

A benefit, on the other hand, is something more subtle. A benefit is what the product can do for the prospect -- how it can make his or her life better, how it can save time, how it can enhance prestige, how it can make life fun and easy, and more. So, a benefit is not a thing -- it is an aspect of the customer's life that is made better.

Benefits come from features, which is why this confuses some people. For example, let us say a car has a 230-horsepower engine. That is a feature. But what does this do for the person who buys the car? A powerful engine helps the driver accelerate with ease on the motorway and easily merge with traffic. It gives the driver the power he or she needs to pull a heavy trailer. It gives a feeling of pleasure to have all that mechanical power at the command of one's fingertips. All of these are benefits -- something the customer feels gets or is satisfied by.

And this is what you should sell - the benefits.
Benefits are what people really care about. They want to know how their lives will be made better by the product more than what the product is made of, or what its design specs are. When you spend too much time talking about your product's features, you run the risk of "me oriented" selling rather than focusing on customer needs. You cannot assume that a prospect will naturally see how they benefit just because you describe your product physically.

It is much smarter to keep the focus on the customer
- on his or her needs, desires, longings, problems, demands - and then paint a picture that clearly and vibrantly shows the customer how they can get all of the above if they buy your product. It's known as 'selling the sizzle and not the steak.

When you only list details about features, you do not do that, even though it may seem like you are. Look at the following example:

> "Our premium chair is upholstered with the finest mountain ram's leather which is hand-selected and hand- stitched to an all cherry wood frame. The chair reclines to a 56-degree position, yet preserves a compact position that takes up less space than a normal chair twice its size…"

It sounds fairly good, but it's all features. Ram's leather is great, and cherry wood is nice - but how does the customer benefit? You cannot assume the customer will know, so you have to spell it out for him or her by describing benefits, as in:

Our ergonomic chair is designed with your comfort in mind - the 56 degree reclining position gives strong support to your lower back, meaning you never experience back pain and are able to rest for hours on end without the need to fidget, adjust or change seats.
Our fine mountain ram's leather upholstery feels like heaven against your skin - you experience relaxation with a sense of luxury, and your guests will be impressed by the rich look and sense of

style afforded your living room..."

Here we see how the customer clearly benefits - physical comfort, no back aches from sitting too long, gaining a feeling of pride or prestige from guests who admire your excellent choice of home furnishings.

Never list, use or describe a feature without also telling potential buyers just how that feature will affect them in their real lives, how it will improve their lives, how it will enhance personal comfort, deliver a feeling of pride, satisfaction, gain, and so on.

A great way to discover what your product benefits are is to make a "You get" list. Write down "You get" 10 times on a sheet of paper, and then name specific benefits to follow each "You get." If you write, "You get a 230-horsepower engine..." you have listed a feature.

That is not enough. Complete the process by also saying, "You get a powerful 230 HP engine that never leaves you stuck or sluggish at a roundabout and thrills you when you take tight curves on a carefree drive in the country..."

Just remember - a feature is most often some physical aspect of your products, but the benefit is all about the customer and what the customer gets, experiences and is satisfied by. The latter - benefits - is what really sells.

XBS Principle 14

Reactivating Your Past Customers

If something cost you, say, R100,000 in marketing expense to obtain, would it make sense to just ignore it and never use it after you paid for it? Of course not, but that is what a lot of business owners do all the time. We are talking about your list of past customers, and lapsed customers.

Each name on that list represents every Rand you ever spent on advertising, direct mail, and publicity, and all the hours upon hours of your time spent creating those ads, or doing the networking, or writing the sales letters, and everything else you do to capture customers and get them into your data base.

Furthermore, it costs from eight to ten times as much to go out and find new customers, so your past customer list becomes even more valuable not only because you already "have" them, but also because your past customers already know you, have bought from you before, which makes them far more likely to buy from you again

Do not think of them as "past" customers. Think of them as "inactive" customers with the potential to come back and buy from you again today and many more times in the future. But they will not do it on their own - not most of the time. No, you have to get proactive and start working that customer list with a solid plan and goals for creating more sales using those valuable names.

First, if you have not contacted the names on your customer list for a long time, or if a lot of those customers have not come back to you on their own for a long time, you need to institute a "lost customer reactivation strategy."

One of the best ways to get old customers back is with a letter. We are not talking about a normal sales letter here, but actually a special kind of sales letter called a "reactivation letter."

Such letters take a somewhat personal tone that appeals to emotions or uses slight humor to break the ice. For example, your reactivation letter can have a headline with something like:

"Wanted: Information Regarding Missing Customer. Reward Offered." Another approach is more direct. It starts out with: "We miss you! We want you back!"

In the text of the letter, remind the customer that you consider them just that - "a valued customer" - and that you want them back. Give them a reason why they should come back and sweeten it with a great offer in the form an incentive or reward for coming back, such as a discount or something free.

Be sure to ask them to take action, and you may also want to put a time limit on your incentive offer. Make sure the letter has a good kicker in a well-crafted P.S. - the "P.S." is the item in sales letters which gets read the most, tons of studies have shown.

There is nothing wrong with getting on the telephone and calling the names on your past customer list as well. Do not make the called unscripted, however. This is a "we want you back call" but it is also a structured sales call that will make an offer and ask the past customer to take specific action.

You should also be prepared to tell the customer why they should come back, how they can do it if they need to know (if they have forgotten your address or phone number, which is almost a certainty), and what and how they can expect to benefit for doing what you want them to do - come back.

Of course, many of your past customers will have reasons for not coming back - sometimes good reasons - and you must be prepared to counter these reasons, fix the problem, or provide a solution to whatever it is that is preventing the customer from buying again.

For example, a newspaper is calling lapsed customers to re-subscribe. They get the following reasons for not accepting, but they have anticipated them and have ready-to-go answers:

The experienced marketer is ready for objections and reasons not to buy and have an answer ready to counter.

When you do provide an exceptionally good alternative to their problem, it becomes exceedingly difficult for the customer not to agree and then say yes.

Another inducement to get a customer back is to offer them a one-time super deal that is too good to turn down. Here is an example of how you might accomplish this with a letter:

Dear Customer:

We have been thinking about you lately, we miss you, and we've decided that we really want you back a valued customer.

In the past, you purchased our standard road breakdown plan that provided you with complete roadside assistance in the event your car breaks down and leaves you stranded.

For R99 a year, you were assured of receiving emergency towing service, car rental discounts, 15% off on all your hotel stays, free traveler's cheques, free maps and route planning performed by our travel experts, discounts on plane tickets, and more.

Because we want you back, and because we want to make sure all your travel experiences are safe and worry free, you can get all the same coverage for one year at just half of what paid for it the first time - just R49 for all the great coverage you get with the regular R99 a year plan.

Why are we willing to give you such a steep discount? We simply want to win your business back. We make no bones about it.

We know once you experience the safety, confidence, and discount savings of being fully covered by our hazard and roadside assistance service, you will never want to be without it again.

Remember that if you take advantage of our hotel and place ticket discounts, you can easily recapture the cost of your premium. Also, towing service today has never been more expensive.

If your car needs to be towed just 10 miles, the cost can be in excess of R200. We do not want you to break down and be stranded somewhere, but if it happens, R49 premium means you don't have to worry about some super expensive towing bill, and other charges associated with car problems.

Reinstating your plan has never been easier. Simply call our freephone number at the bottom of this letter and tell our representative that you want our special R49 Return Customer deal, and you will be covered immediately.

No need to send money now; we will bill you later. Or you can pay with a credit card over the phone or detach and send in the card we have provided for you below.

If you choose to rejoin us within 10 days, you will also receive a complimentary World Road Atlas which included detailed maps of every major and minor road in the country, and is also packed with the names and addressed of all the best travel destinations, best hotels, including their phone numbers, along with a lot of other information. The Atlas sells retail for R19.95 but it is your free for coming back to us as a customer at half price, just R49.00.

You can also cancel your plan at any time and get a full refund of your premium, but you still get to keep the Road Atlas simply for coming back to us and trying our service again.

We hope to hear from you today. This is a risk-free offer with a full money-back guarantee, so you have nothing to lose. A representative is ready to take your call right now, and thanks in advance for taking the time to consider this one- time offer, and thanks for your past business.

Good Luck and Happy Travelling, Sincerely,

Joe Smith
Acme Roadside Service.

Yet another effective means of reinvigorating old customers is to call them and tell you are contacting them to give them advanced notice of a special, unadvertised sale. Tell them that as a past and valued customer, you want them to be among an exclusive list of people who are being invited to get some spectacular discounts which will not be available to the general public.

It also helps to offer some truly spectacular deals at the sale - so not only do you appeal to the past customer's personal prestige by treating him or her like an "insider" and a "preferred customer," you sweeten the deal by offering true value and real savings on something they have demonstrated an interest in buying in the past - because they bought from you in the past! I would also encourage you to keep mailing your lapsed customers for as long as you know their address is good, and for as long as you know the customer is still with the living. Experienced direct response marketers know that people often buy only after receiving five to 10 mailings.

If a customer bought from you once, keep mailing them your regular materials, and keep doing it for several years, even if they rarely or never respond. It is still worth doing so because a large enough percentage will respond sooner or later and make your effort worthwhile. Also, remember that any mailing can be made much stronger if you follow it up with a phone call.

The ways in which you can bring back lapsed customers in limited only by your marketing imagination. The bottom line is - your past customer list and your lapsed customer list is almost certainly a far richer source of future business than customers you have yet to attract and sell. You still need to continue your efforts to find new customers to constantly build your data base of names - but once you have those names, get the most out of them by never giving up on them.

XBS Principle 15

Follow Up to Even Greater Success

"Persistence is what makes the impossible possible, the possible likely and the likely definite." - Robert Half, Personnel Executive

Whenever a prospect comes into your sphere of influence - into your store, calls you on the phone, requests more information by mail, and whether they buy anything or not - you must latch onto that person like a barnacle on a whale. You think that is a bad metaphor?

Well, maybe it is, but think of this: a barnacle is not a parasite to a whale. They actually help the whale out. It's what biologists call a "symbiotic relationship." That is when two organisms get together and benefit each other. Barnacles help keep the outer skin of the whale smooth and free of harmful build-ups of unwanted algae and other stuff that could harm the whale's skin and prevent the giant mammal from moving smoothly through the water. The barnacle wins, too, because it likes to eat all that nasty build-up on the outer surface of the whale.

This admittedly belabored example explains the kind of relationship you should develop with your clients, customers, and contacts. Latch onto them and never let them go and let them help you by paying you money as you provide them with products and services that make their lives better.

The key is persistence. Never consider any contact a one-shot deal. When you sell a person once, enter that person's name in your customer data base and plan for ways to make future sales. Continued contact will pay off in the long run if you persistently pursue them with future offers.

Here is why you must keep following up:

The Moving Parade – The Irresistible Customer Relationship Model
We have already talked about this earlier in these pages. People are constantly in a state of change. If they do not want or need what you have today, it's very possible that they'll need it tomorrow, next week, or next month.

So, giving up after only one or two tries or after a week or two will be definition mean failure. Sometimes people do not buy today because maybe they're short on cash at the moment. But that could be different on another day.

If you hit a person on pay-day, or at the opportune time you may easily make the sale. Remember that people's needs, wants and situations constantly change, which is a good reason to keep following up.

Going Down the Ladder of Greater Sales

Keeping up the follow up means going back to clients with additional offers again, again and again. Let me give you an example to explain what this means:

A company I know offers internet-based business opportunities. It sends out direct mailings offering a video or manual for R50 (actually R49.97) to lists that it rents. Of say a list of 30,000, it will typically get a response of 2%, that is 600 sales – at R50 – they make R30,000. Now that is okay but for these numbers and the high cost of acquisition (postage, list rental, mailing piece, fulfilment, warehousing, administration, etc), it's not fantastic.
Sometimes a company may do this as a loss leader - You will see why…

Next, they send out a different and bigger offer within four weeks - just to the one is that bought.

Remember, these are now customers who have already displayed their trust and keen interest by buying the first item.

They are a qualified customer buying list. Anyway, in this new mailing, they offer a home study course costing R400 (R397). The response rate is higher - 10% - because they are now selling hotdogs to a hungry crowd. That is 60 sales at R400 – They make R24,000. Less money you say, but the cost of acquisition and fulfilment is much less, and they now have a qualified 'house list'.

Then, they offer a one-day seminar with lots of bonuses and 'secrets' on offer for R3,000 (R2,997). They aim this particularly to the ones that bought the R400 item and once again the response is 10%. That is 6 sales at R3,000. They make R18,000 for much less acquisition cost and big reward. It is nearly all profit.

It goes without saying that they use many lists to concurrently (and/or repeat) this process.

You may not be offering videos, manual and courses but you can apply the very same concept to your selling efforts, no matter what you sell. The same formula applies. You make an initial offer to a large group of people, and of course, it helps if that offer is a fantastic deal.

The ones that buy have automatically qualified themselves as potentially hot buyers of even more expensive items. You can keep working those same numbers, going down the ladder, making ever smaller, numbers of sales - but of higher profit items that earn you even better profits than selling a lot of low-priced items to greater numbers of people.

XBS Principle 16

Guarantees - Remove the Risk and Make Sales

Experienced marketers know: People's resistance to buy is always high. We are conditioned that way - to be wary. Just think of those times you may have been burned on some purchase. This kind of experience sticks in the minds of buyers. They remember the sting of being "had."

Also, most people know that advertisers often stretch or bend the truth, if not outright lie. We are taught from the time we're young to be wary shoppers, and to "always look for the best deal."

And that is the way it should be. If we did not shop with both eyes open, we'd all be nothing more than a bunch of suckers. The trouble is, when somebody like you is offering a product of true quality and solid benefits, easily worth the price you are asking, you still have to deal with that same healthy skepticism.

Therefore, you have to overcome natural resistance to buy. The more you do to put prospects at ease, the more they will buy from you.

The primary way to eliminate this perceived risk is to reverse that risk onto yourself. That most often means an unconditional money-back guarantee. You get the product back and the customer gets their money back - that is it!

Of course, you also need to really sell the guarantee and make the customer know for certain that they are risking nothing by doing business with you.

There are other ways to reduce resistance to buying. One of the best is delaying payment - letting the customer buy now and pay later. You have probably seen some furniture sellers and computer stores offering deals like this: "No payments and no interest for 6 months!" You may not want to go that far, but it certainly works to stimulate sales.

A stronger guarantee is to offer the product on a validation guarantee. In other words, they only pay if it does what you say it will do.

Still another way to reduce buying resistance is to make buying easier for the customer by offering multiple payment methods. Credit cards, payment plans, no

money down, personal cheque, cash - the more ways you let them buy, and the easier you make it, the more ways they will.

One of the best forms of guarantee is the 'Better Than Money Back" or "Better Than Risk Free". This works by not only offering the customer their money back but also, they get to keep any bonuses or 'freebies' that were offered with the product or service. These bonuses should be low cost to you but high perceived value to the customer. So, when initially making the offer, you should also articulate the value of the bonuses, i.e. 'When you buy this product, you will also get these bonuses worth over R130 and even if you decide to get your money back, you'll still be R130 better off just for trying our product'.

A lot of businesspeople just do not like the idea of a "no questions asked" or "better than risk free" money back guarantee. It scares them.

They think they will be taken advantage of by unscrupulous buyers, and yes, it does happen. But the bottom line is this: Your sales will increase so dramatically when you offer surprisingly risk-free buying options, your profits will more than cover that small percentage of sales that obligate you to honour your refund offer.

Also, when you treat your customers right, they will come back to you again and again, even if they initially ask for a reference they'll know you're an honest dealer and you stand by your product and by your word. That kind of reputation spreads fast, and that means lots of positive word-of-mouth advertising which brings lots of new customer referrals.

Also, if you are offering true quality and are delivering on what your advertising promises, your return rates will be small. So, sell quality and reverse the risk back it up with an iron-clad guarantee. It works.

XBS Principle 17

Capturing Customers Details

A list of customer names in an extremely valuable commodity to anyone selling anything. Names, addresses and phone numbers of qualified clients are big business in themselves. If you have ever dealt with a professional list broker, you know what We are talking about. A one- time rental of an extremely hot, clean list of 5,000 names can cost a minimum of R750, but very often a lot more.

While you can go out and pay good money to buy lists, you also have the power to create your own. Every customer who answers your ads, responds to your sales letter, or comes into your store has a name, and you should have a system in place for not only capturing that name, but all additional data associated with that name as you can muster.

Gathering names that is keyed to buying behavior has become a high-tech science but is also somewhat controversial. Laser scanners in check-out lines, for example, can automatically capture all of the information on a customer's credit card and store it electronically. It can also key customer names to specific products they buy.

So when a person goes to the same supermarket over a period of several months, an entire data base of that person's buying behavior can be automatically tracked and stored in customer list files, which marketers can then examine at their leisure for the purpose of shaping and directing future marketing messages at those individuals.

I say it is somewhat controversial because, increasingly, privacy issues are involved. Some people feel uncomfortable with major or even minor corporations that are subtly and automatically building up detailed personality profiles on individuals by tracking their buying habits and behaviors.
Also, the crime of identity theft is the fastest growing kind of offence in the world. Because of this, people are increasingly leery of giving personal information and additional data about themselves to anyone, including honest people like ourselves who only want to sell them good products and services.

Taking all of this into account, you should still have a plan to capture as many names as possible and build your own customer list and data base. Computer technology makes it easier than ever before. Ask your software and computer dealer for the equipment you need to capture and manage customer information.

A personal touch still has a place in our world as well, however. That means getting your salespeople to ask people for their names and addresses, along with the strong reassurance that you will never sell, share, or use their personal information for anything other than for interaction with your business. The majority of people are still glad to do it.

Direct mail is an easy way to capture names and other vital information because people need to fill out your order form and list all of their information when they send it in to buy.

But another good way to capture names is to run contests and conduct surveys. Many people will happily fill out your form in exchange for a chance to win something of value. When you use a survey, you can combine valuable marketing research efforts with gathering names.

Have a plan for gathering names and building a customer mailing list. Ask any experienced, successful marketer and he or she will tell you - their "house mailing list" is their most precious commodity. Indeed arguably, the most valuable asset in any business is the customer list and, as has been discussed in other chapters, the closeness of the relationship that the business has to that customer list.
Working the list consistently, can be a source of incredible income for years to come.

XBS Principle 18

Boosting Sales with Bonuses

Including a "bonus" to make what your selling gain greater value, while at the same time costing you very little, is a powerful way to generate more sales, command higher prices and make your customers happier all at the same time.

Your challenge is to find a product, service or some aspect of something that can be added on, included or built into what your selling, with the most important element being the perception on behalf of the customer that they are getting something extra - a great deal.

Computer dealers, for example, often "bundle" software and include it with the purchase of a computer. In fact, doing so costs little, or perhaps nothing, except the price of a few CDs on which the software is encoded. But the perceived value can be enormous.

Perhaps you can offer a free book, consultation or even a free extended warranty. As stated earlier, as few as 12% of actual buyers end up using the extended warranty, making your risk small, but the boost to your sales is significant.

Remember, your bonus offering does not necessarily have to be something tangible - as an extended warranty - but give the feel and perception that what is being purchased is a better, enhanced deal.

XBS Principle 19

Having A Back End

If you have a nice back end, you are going to make a lot of money in sales. No, we are talking about that back- end! We are talking about a selling strategy that you simply must adopt right now - the very survival of your business may depend on it. What is back-ending? Simply this: It means having a second, third, maybe even a fourth product ready to sell after right after you make the first sale. This is the way real money is made in sales, and sometimes, it is the only way a true profit is made.

Amazingly, many businesses do not do this.

Finding first-time customers is expensive. You have to advertise, send direct mail pieces, pay salespeople salaries or commissions, and bear the cost of telemarketing and more. Then tack on your other overhead costs, such as labour, raw materials, or what you pay wholesale for your retail sale items. Then calculate the time, agony, and effort in getting that customer to put trust in your service or product - only to sell to them just once. What a waste!

Add it all up and each customer you attract, and sell can cost as much or more than the profit you make from each sale.

The solution is to make additional sales to each customer you have already bought and paid for with your marketing efforts. Each time you sell more to that customer, it frees you from the need to pay more to find a new customer -- although you still need to keep doing that on an ongoing basis.

But the point is, once you have a customer, get the most out of him or her because you have expended a lot of resources to find that person in the first place.

Successful back-ending means careful planning. It means having additional products ready to go and available at the time of the first sale. Back-ending works best when you try to make that second or third sale right away, and not two weeks later when the customer has already cooled off, or even maybe forgotten about you.

If you sell shoes, also be ready to sell shoe polish, and maybe a pair of socks. If you sell a shirt, sell a tie, or several ties. If you sell bicycles, sell as many accessories as you can - water bottles, pumps, biking gear, such as shoes, gloves, caps and more. If you sell computers, sell software and an extended warranty.

It is really a simple concept to make back-end sales, but it is amazing how many sellers never do it. Even if you're satisfied with the profits you're making on your first sale right now, and you don't think you need a second-tier product, think about how much potential income you're letting pass by, possibly to go into your competitors pockets.

Back ending is the method to continually garnering continuing profits from the customers that you have spent so much money acquiring and worked so hard to get.

So, take care of your back end, and it will take care of you.

XBS Principle 20

Testimonials

Positive testimonials about your product given by past, satisfied customers are one of the most powerful tools known in marketing, and you cannot afford not to incorporate testimonials into all your ads, sales letters, brochures and more.

Testimonials are powerful tools of persuasion. Here is why: In the eyes of potential buyers, a testimonial is much like having a trusted friend recommend your product.

A testimonial is that part of the ad - perhaps the only part - that does not seem like just a little more ad hype.

That is because the message of a testimonial is not coming from the seller himself. Customers know that businesses will say just about anything to make a sale. Everyone has a well-developed, "Let the buyer beware" mentality when he or she confront ads and sales pitches. We all naturally and habitually cast a skeptical eye on most ad claims. We are on the constant lookout for deception.

But a testimonial from a "real person" is different. When a potential buyer reads or sees a testimonial from an "ordinary" person, he or she gets the feeling they are receiving an endorsement straight from the horse's mouth, so to speak. And they are! That is the beauty of a testimonial. When an objective, third party individual, who has no financial interest in your company, is willing to put his or her reputation on the line to promote your product, it says a lot about how good that products really must be.

Testimonials "prove" that your product is as good as you say it is. It shows potential buyers that others have already tried and tested the product and found it good enough to go out and brag about it and tell others to buy it. When a customer confronts a testimonial, he or she thinks: "Hey, it worked for him, so maybe can work for me, too!" You cannot beat that kind of endorsement.

The best testimonials are made by people who are or appear to be in the same demographic group as your potential buyers. This way, the testimonial endorsement appears to be coming from a known and trusted person. Testimonials made by well-known people or admired celebrities are also powerful persuaders.

If you do not have any testimonials for your product or service, go out and get them. Contact satisfied customers and ask them simply to tell what they liked about your product, and how they benefited from it.

Have them sign their testimonial statement and get their permission to use it in all your marketing mediums. If you can include a picture or live video tape of satisfied customers making a pitch for you, all the better.

Keep all of your signed permission editorials on file for future use and reference. And because you must have proof of permission to use another person's statement in your advertising media. Also, get both a first and last name to use in your testimonials. Testimonials that are signed, "Mike K., Glasgow" can easily seem faked or simply made up, (and they often are!) Customers are wise to that.

Even if you are a brand-new business and have yet to create a satisfied customer, you should strive to get testimonials you can use. These can come from people you know and who are familiar with your product.

But whatever you do, use testimonials! No marketing vehicle is complete without at least one.

XBS Principle 21

The Exit Strategy

Every business owner should have an exit strategy.
Unfortunately for many, the reality is to be found slumped over the desk having had a fatal heart attack.

The main purpose of the business should be to sell it at a tremendous windfall profit. If you are a business owner, you should create a three-year exit plan. In other words, in three years' time you are either going to sell it, float it or franchise it. If you do not wish to do any of those then you must pretend that you will.

Why? Because in the process of making it ready to sell, the business gets streamlined, making it more efficient, systemized and with proper processes, policies, and procedures in place.

Remember, that the definition of a business is an entity that runs itself. You should not have to be at the premises all the time for the business to work. Think about it, if you have to be in your business all the time for it to run, you probably don't really have a business – what you have is a job.

For the exit strategy… Buyers or investors want to buy a business that can seemingly run itself. They want a going concern – not necessarily a job.

The problem with many business owners is that they try to sell a business that is not finished and therefore end up getting only a fraction of its true value.

You must make the business ready to sell by spending some time in revamping, or in many cases creating a Policies and Procedures Manual. This manual will be viewed by the astute buyer as the 'instruction' book to run the company – and so it is!

Finally, there are two kinds of money: income and capital. Very few people get rich from income – The way to wealth is capital and the realization of capital can be achieved through selling, floating, or franchising the business.

XBS System Module 2

Fast Cash Tactics

8 Fast Cash Tactics to Flood Your Business with Money Now

Introduction

Many businesses hit a dead spell now and then. Suddenly, the cash flow slows down like blood flowing through an artery blocked with cholesterol! Lots of things can cause this... A downturn in the economy, a bunch of ads that did not pull, new competition stealing your business.

Stalled cash flow is no reason for panic, but it can certainly be a motivator to get busy and do something about it. Indeed, a serious slowdown may be just the wake-up call needed to breathe new life into your business.

The quick, simple, and yet enormously powerful fast cash generating Tactics detailed here can be used to give a rapid profit boost, thereby highlighting, and enhancing your business expertise and reputation.

The great news is that your business like 99% of other businesses is perfect for these Tactics providing you have one vital thing: Hidden Assets that are under- utilised. These assets include past customer lists, current customer database, advertising opportunities, salespeople, and telemarketing, etc.

What we especially like about all these fast cash Tactics is they are great for bringing in a torrent of money almost immediately plus they work all year round. They are all proven Tactics that should become part of your overall business building strategy.

Okay, let us get started.

Fast Cash Strategy 1

Gift Certificates & Gifting the Gift Giver

The Company Cash idea is really a kind of gift certificate, which brings us to another cash boosting idea: The gift certificate.

Many may be already selling gift certificates, but perhaps in the same boring old way. You might have an advertisement, or a sign posted in your store that says: "Gift Certificates available." – which is nothing more than a statement of fact. It is not proactive and does nothing to motivate large numbers of people to buy a gift certificate right away. So, here is how to inject some real life and excitement into the idea ...

Put together a special mailing piece which is sent to your customers. In it, explain that you realize and understand that gift giving is a chore and a painful obligation to some people, and you have the perfect way to get all your Christmas shopping or birthday shopping or anniversary shopping taken care of right away, and without effort. Let them know that you offer gift certificates year-round or say you have decided to begin offering gift certificates now because you have never done it before.

Here is a sample letter you can send out (please see next page) ...

```
Dear Preferred Customer,

   Have you ever scrambled at the last minute to get your
Christmas shopping done before it's too late?  Have you fought
your way through busy shopping malls, battled other shoppers in
the store, or felt overwhelmed by your need to get your gift
shopping out of the way?

   Or maybe you have no idea what to get your wife, husband,
or friend for their birthday, anniversary or special occasion
this year?

   Well, we understand how you feel.  That's why we offer gift
certificates as a convenience to our best customers.
Better yet, we have chosen this non- holiday time to write to
you about gift certificates because we have a deal for you!
     Normally our gift certificates sell for face value, but
now for a short time, we are offering a 15% discount on gift
certificates as a special offer to you!

   Also, for every R50 gift certificate you buy, we'll give you
a R5 gift certificate you can treat yourself with right now!
                         So why not get the
gift-shopping monkey off your back right now and get free R5
certificates to spend on yourself (or someone else).

   Hurry!  The offer ends in 7 days!  We look forward to
seeing you soon!

Sincerely,


Mike Businessman
```

Making the gift certificate offer sweeter with a bribe is an incredibly powerful strategy. It is impossible for an offer like that to NOT get a great response! Best of all, you get cash coming in fast.

Here is another super gift certificate twist: Approach a business with a large number of employees and offer to sell them a stack of gift certificates they can hand out to their employees next Christmas at bonus time. Many companies offer year-end or holiday bonuses anyway.
You can cash in now by letting the company get this task behind them by purchasing gift certificates from you at a discount. This can be an amazingly easy way to make a few hundred, or a few thousand sales in a single day, and get an injection of cash flow that may solve all your capital needs instantly.

Selling paper in the forms of contract pre-purchase discounts, company cash, or gift certificates is a fast way to generate cash flow. But be careful… Do not forget to keep your future fulfilment costs in mind. When the paper starts coming in to redeem purchases, you must have the stock on hand to complete the deal.

Fast Cash Strategy **2**

Reactivate Past Customers

This is an immensely powerful, quick, and simple strategy that works by seemingly raising the dead.

Many businesses see their past customers as a lost cause, so much so that they completely set them aside, forget about or totally ignore the opportunity that they present.

And yet, past customers are a high profit, hidden asset lying within a business just waiting to be picked up and utilised and can produce massive sources of easy revenue and here is why… It is said that it is eight times easier to sell to existing clients than it is to new clients.

This is because you are appealing to people that you know need your product or service, instead of running say an expensive ad to attract new customers that may reach a lot of people who may not be interested in your offer….

And here lies the opening - By writing out to your past customers with a special offer you have the perfect opportunity to reactivate them.

Depending upon the type of business, product, or service you offer, the revenues generated by this technique can literally flood your business with profits at low acquisition cost within a noticeably short period of time.

Re-establishing contact with your past customers is an easy yet effective strategy. Customers cease to be customers for a variety of reasons:
- They may have become disgruntled with a member of staff, price, service, delivery, etc.
- Perhaps they found a cheaper source, or their needs changed.
- Maybe they moved away.

There are any number of reasons but what remains consistent is human responsiveness to a simple appeal.

Here is all you do… Write a letter, similar to that below, and post it out to your past customers and literally wait for the stampede.

If Bribes Are Illegal, Mr. Smith…
We are Willing to Break the Law to Get You Back!

That is how much you mean to us… and that is why I've enclosed a special Discount Voucher with this letter.

When we do not see our good customers for a while, it concerns us, and raises a few questions. Did something happen to you? Are you okay? Are you still in business? Did we do something wrong, or something to upset or offend you?

Because you are a valued customer and it has been a while since you've been in to see us, we're offering you a special "bribe" to get you back.

I am sure you remember us a friendly and locally owned family company where you are always sure of a warm welcome and a nice cup of tea. But we are really much more than that.

In addition to having a wide array and stock of plant for hire (and for sale): Everything from **Excavators to Compressors, Breakers to Rollers and Dumpers to Fork Lifts plus a lot more,** we can also REPAIR and MAINTAIN *your* large and small plant, garden machinery and even hand tools in our fully equipped workshop facilities or on- site.

And when you include the promise of fast delivery and pickup, our guarantee of reliability on all our plant and machinery (if there's a problem - we're there for you) and honest to goodness value for money… all coupled with the best prices around, I'm sure you'll admit that we offer

quite an impressive package for your plant hire needs.

Now throw in the enclosed Discount Voucher (we call it an "ethical bribe"), that entitles you to a **BIG 10% off** for 2 Days hire, a **MASSIVE 15% off** for 3 Days hire, or even a **WHOPPING GREAT 20% off** for hire of 4 days or more, and you'd almost have to be a fool to pass it up!

If you will book and pay for two days or more of plant hire before September 30th, you will get the special prices, and the savings go straight into your bank account!

So please give us another try… just give us a call on 01234 567890, or drop by… I know you will be pleasantly surprised!

Kind regards, Mike Jones

P.S. This is a **genuine discount**, no preloaded or artificial prices and way below our competitors… The kettle's on and we would love to welcome you back soon.

Fast Cash Strategy **3**

Bring Dead Inventory to Life

If you have got dead inventory, you've got several problems in one. First, you have money tied up in that inventory, money you could be putting to good use.
Second, you may be paying to store it. Third, the longer it sits, the more its value may fade, especially if it is a perishable or degradable product. And more.

So, it makes sense to move this stuff out. That may mean slashing prices till it hurts -- but if that gets the stuff moving and brings in cash, you are better off in the long run. Sometimes it is better to lose some profit in exchange for good old liquid cash, which you can use to bolster advertising, direct mail and other marketing efforts.

Another idea for dead inventory: Start giving it away free! Why? Because you can tie that freebie to sales of other products. Use your dead inventory as a sales stimulus to get your entire operation going.

Now here are a dozen more creative dead inventory ideas:

1. Instead of trying to sell the stuff one item at a time, offer the whole shooting match to someone for one, low price. You eliminate inventory immediately and get some needed cash.

This has the added advantage of not having to advertise or spend money on direct marketing. Just make some calls, make a great deal, and unload the inventory.

Who will buy it? Another business might. If the price is really low, how about a charity or non-profit organisation? When you sell to a charity, you get some cash, and also build your image as a business with a heart. Offer your entire load to a charity or non-profit organisation at one rock-bottom price.

2. How about an overseas market? With a couple of phone calls, you might be able to move the stuff to

another country. What does not sell fast here may blaze off the shelves as an export product.

3. Trade dead inventory for advertising. Why not approach a media provider and give them your inventory in exchange for some ads? You might be able to work out a deal.

4. Look for another company that is looking for a "free gift" idea for one of their own promotions. Give them a great deal on your dead inventory, and you will both wins. Look for a company that would be a good "fit" for what you want to unload.

5. Barter it. Trade your dead inventory for some other kind of inventory you feel you can sell more easily.

6. Try a tandem mailing with a compatible company. Do a co-operative mailing while sharing the postal and shipping expense. The benefits of this method are many.

Each company will gain the advantage of accessing the other's mailing list. If things go well, the right combination of products will stimulate sales for both of you.

Both you and the other company should do better than you would with individual mailings. Advertising costs can also be shared.

7. Small Lots: If your dead inventory consists of small lots of several different items, maybe your best bet would be to make connections with a person who sells at open public markets, "crazy day" sales, car boot sales, or even flea markets.

Large scale flea-marketer developers are always scavenging for items to market cheap. They will jump at the chance to pick up your generously discounted items.

8. If you have larger stocks of discontinued items, look for a wholesaler who supplies flea-marketers, or dirt. Cheap bulk and warehouse dealers who open their doors to the general public.

Do not forget large retail "buying club" type operations. These outlets offer basement floor prices to the public, especially if they buy in large quantities. Call them up and make a deal and get the dead weight out of your cargo hold!

9. Here is another idea using charities or other organizations looking to raise funds: Print up door drop leaflets announcing fantastic discounts on a number of short stock items.

Then arrange for a local charity or public organisation to get volunteers to spread out and distribute your door drop leaflets. Offer the volunteer organisation a percentage of the sales.

Make sure your leaflets tell people this is a fund raiser and that you are being a good corporate citizen by helping out.

You move dead inventory and strike a blow for you image at the same time. The leaflet could also serve as an order blank to complete the whole process at once.

10. You could also get your charity organisation partners to come in and staff a bank of phones set up to take orders, and also make sales calls offering terrific deals "for charity." The volunteers could also handle distribution and delivery.

11. Sell the stuff to employees of other companies. Find a business with a large number of employees. Then make arrangement with management to offer your inventory "exclusively" to their employees.

If you have to, cut the host company in on some profits. You may be able to move a few hundred or thousands of widgets this way in just a day, or two.

If you tell the employees who are targeted that some of the money will go to a favorite charity, you will boost sales even more.

12. Offer a local retailer a no-risk consignment deal. They promote the item in their ads and in their stores and you get paid only for what they actually sell.

This means they do not have the risk of purchasing in advance and their advertising costs will be minimal because they can incorporate the products into their regular ads.

It is an attractive deal for them, and whatever they sell will be gravy for you since you have virtually no distribution and advertising costs!

13. Auction it! Why not hold a public auction? A professional auctioneer will take care of all the details for a cut of the sales.

With an auction, you may not, of course, be able to dictate a price, but you may get even more than you originally hoped for sometimes!

A skilled, professional auctioneer can often get more for items than you would sell them for at discount. The auction agent will also take care of all the advertising for the big event. (Be sure to give them a list of people or businesses that you think should be notified.)

Another advantage of an auction is that you can use the opportunity to sell things other than your dead inventory.

You can sell other stuff along with it and have a big day for cash flow! Do not forget to put a marketing message -- brochure, coupon, sales piece -- in the hand of every person who attends the auction!

Fast Cash Strategy 4
Contact Your Loyal Customers

If you want to jump start cash flow, get out your customer lists and offer a special promotion to your best customers.

Present this new promotion as an invitation only "appreciation sale' for your "exclusive supporters." Offer a generously discounted price, but make sure you offer it only to your best, repeat customers.

But as you give them a good discount, there is no reason why you cannot up-sell them at the same time or make a back-end sale! If they are your best customers, you will have a big chance of making good sales.

When you do your appreciation sale and offer a great deal, make sure you:

- Show them in black and white what they are saving over original cost.
- Show how you are beating a competitor's price.
- Make sure they know they are the ONLY ONES getting the deal.

You can also give it a party atmosphere by adding cocktails, balloons, etc.

By giving extra special attention to select customers, you build their loyalty and keep them coming back. They also spend more money than other customers.

You can afford to put more time and resources into such customers because each may have the value of 10 or 20 "ordinary" customers. It is a truth of business that 80% of your business comes from 20% of your customers.

With this in mind, it only makes sense to treat that highly valuable 20% like they are special to you -- because they are!

Using the power of telemarketing as either the primary method of approach or as a follow-up can put a rocket under the response to this strategy.

Fast Cash Strategy 5

A Deal For Your Other Customers

After your special promotion to your cream of the crop customers, get out the rest of the mailing lists and send everyone some kind of lesser deal. Explain to them exactly why you are doing this. Reason may include:

- The truth! We are doing this to bolster fast cash flow!
- Business is slow, so you, the customers benefits!
- You just got a great one-time only buy on a bunch of stuff and you want to pass on the savings!
- You have to raise cash or lay off employees soon! Please help us keep our people employed! With your help, we can do it!
- This is the slow season and so we are offering a deal to generate cash.
- Make sure you tell them the deal will be GONE when business picks up again!

Even if the reason seems a bit negative, such as your business is in cash flow trouble, just telling it like it is can give you an honest, matter-of-fact image that customers can understand and appreciate.

It is like your levelling with a friend. You are making a frank statement and hoping for the best.

Note: Some may correctly dissent on this. There may be a lot of businesspeople who would not admit they were in trouble if they were down to their last cent!

The thought is that the public will see the company as a failure waiting to happen, and no one likes a loser. Yet, on the other hand, this can give many people the idea that there's great deals to be had because this company is desperate!

But whatever you do, do not whine, or threaten. "You must buy, or we're finished!" Remember, positive oriented marketing almost always trumps negative oriented advertising. So even if your reasons are negative, strive to couch them in a positive light

Fast Cash Strategy **6**

Upsell!

Upselling can be one of the easiest, quickest, and simplest cash fixes available. Here is a few ideas:

1. The first thing that you can do is to introduce a handy phrase that can be used by your sales staff as a prompt to garner a larger or add-on sale from customers.

'McDonalds are masters of this strategy, who isn't familiar with; 'Would you like fries with that?' or 'Would you like to go large?'

What can you do in your business? You could start by looking at offering a complementary product with every sale.

For instance, dry cleaners could offer a suit cover at a special discount with every purchase. A printer could offer an express delivery or service for a little extra.

A hotel could offer a luxury pack of champagne, flowers and chocolates, a movie, or an upgrade in room. Another thought is to encourage customers to buy more by offering a special bonus item with every purchase above RX amount.

2. A familiar upsell tactic is 'buy one and get one free'. The airline companies have used this very successfully to tempt back travelers into their fledging business and first-class seats.

Video stores can offer a second movie free or at a lower price. It need not necessarily be the same product. You could also offer a discount on a second or third purchase of the same item to literally multiply your turnover.

3. A variation on this is to offer a discount on the next purchase, thereby securing future custom.

4. You can also bundle or package products (or services) together. Looking again at McDonalds they offer 'meals', which is usually a burger, fries and a drink.

Cosmetics retailers could offer perfume and creams together at a discounted price – or with a free cosmetics bag or lipstick. What can you package together in your business to skyrocket your sales?

Upselling is one of the best methods for turning around falling sales or increasing cash flow. It can have a truly dramatic effect on your profits as in most cases there are no new customer acquisition costs – you're selling more to existing customers and it costs at least eight times more to find a new customer than sell to an existing one.

Fast Cash Strategy 7

Telephone Questionnaires & Prompters

Each and every call that comes into your business has value. You must realize this and make it part of your company philosophy. Every call is not only an opportunity to make a sale, but it can also tell you a great deal about what is going on with your marketing effort.

Using a telephone questionnaire for every incoming call is an amazingly powerful way to convert enquiries to sales - exponentially – just by following the script.

One customer reported that their conversion went from 2 sales out of 10 enquiries to a massive 8 sales out of 10 - just by following the telephone questionnaire sheet. With something like this you can even charge more than your competitors and upsell at the same time. This really is one of the ultimate Fast Cash Tactics!

This strategy is also particularly useful for businesses that operate in a highly competitive market. With this questionnaire you can literally capture the price-oriented enquirer and turn them into a sales closing call or sell them right there on the phone.

Just adapt the questions to your business, put it into action and watch your sales climb.

However, before you use this, here is something else to consider… a secret to selling more. Use this when you are providing quotes or final prices… **Never, ever, reveal the price or details of your product or service without telling them precisely what your product or service will do for them and why you are the only solution.**

That is why the questionnaire is so potent… You will see their responses to your questions, and you can then record these very same responses – the things about your product or service that are important to them – and put them in your quote or proposal to them.

For instance, if you're in the double glazing business and you have a question in your form that asks if they want a 20 year guarantee or special security glass then you would put into the quote or proposal something like:

> "Your new XYZ Co. windows are manufactured with special unbreakable glass that provides you with security and peace of mind". And "Your XYZ Co. windows come with an unprecedented 20-year guarantee that means…"

This is a highly effective strategy – use it!

Qualifying Questionnaire & Phone Script for In-Coming Calls.

For Private Coach Hire

Good morning/afternoon, XYZ Coaches & Tours, This is..How may I help you?

May I take your name please? _____

And your phone numbers? (Work)_____(After Hours)_____

May I ask how you heard about us?_____

Where do you wish to travel to? _____

How many people will be travelling in your party?_____

When were you thinking of going?_____ At what time?_____

How long are you staying?_____What time will you need to be picked up? _____

Are there any pickups en-route? _____

Right that sounds fine, we could take care of you and your party on that day/weekend. I must mention that whilst we are not the most expensive company, we are not the cheapest either. That is because all our coaches are immaculately clean and are fitted with climate control, snug seating, and full toilet & washroom amenities so that you are comfortable and relaxed for the whole journey. Furthermore, we serve complimentary hot and soft drinks to keep you refreshed along the way. A home pick up service can also be made available for a little extra to save you the effort of getting to the couch station. Does that sound like the kind of service that you and your party would enjoy?

I thought so. Now, our Standard Couch service would cost just R ....per person return.

Or you could upgrade to our business class Executive Coaches which would only be an extra R..................................per person return. For that little extra you get lots more legroom, video entertainment, as well as a delicious snack. Which sounds best to you? Great. May I take your

booking now to avoid disappointment?

(IF AVAILABLE ON THE DAY OR IF NO FIRM BOOKING GIVEN):
Just a bit of news for you… We recently acquired the luxurious England Football Team Coach; this is true first-class travel and was used by them for touring right up until 6 months ago. To promote our proud ownership, we are offering a special discount of 20% off the normal rate but as you will appreciate it is booking very fast. Just glancing at the calendar, I have that
date available just at the moment and after the discount it would cost just R… .... per person return. Would you be interested in booking it now to avoid disappointment.

Your address:_____

_____

_____

Thank you, Mr/Mrs/Ms .... we will send out a confirmation letter to you within the next few days.

Qualifying Questionnaire & Phone script for in-coming calls:

Date:_____   First Name:_____&_____

Surname:_____Ph:_____(H)_____(w)

How did you find out about us:_____

Have you had a bitumen driveway constructed before;_____By whom: _____

Were you happy with it? (why yes - why not)_____

When were you thinking of having it done?_____

Do you know how a bitumen driveway is constructed?_____

What sort of soil and drainage do you have on your property? _____

What sort of vehicles use the driveway?_____

When would be the best time to talk to you and your partner, as I have a number of colour options and surface finishes to show you? It may be better if you are both there. I also have a video on how a driveway is made and some examples of finished driveways that we have done. When would be the best time to see you both??

Appointment Date:_____ Day:_____ Time:_____

Notes:_____
_____

How to overcome price shoppers if they insist:

"Well I can give you an approximate price range right now, however the final quote will always depend on the layout of your property, drainage, access to site, soil porosity and type. These are things that I cannot tell you until I see your property and can evaluate the best construction method to suit your property.

I must mention that while we are not the most expensive company, we are not the cheapest either. Our prices range from R8 per square meter to R28 per square meter depending on the soil and type of quality finish you choose. What we aim to do is give you a quality driveway that will suit your property and landscaping colour scheme at a reasonable price. Is that the sort of thing you are after???"

Wait for reply: ____ _ _ _ _ _ _ _ _ _____

"When we come out to see your property, you will also g get the chance to see a video with example of work we have done for others and the different colors and finishes of our driveways."

Notesonsite, colour and finish_____
_____
___ _ _ _ _ _ _ _ _ _ _ _ _ _ Who   took   the   call_____ _ _ _ _ _ _ _ _

Fast Cash Strategy **8**

Flyers

Using flyers is a great way to "deep prospect" a particular geographic area. Flyers have many advantages over letters sent through the mail. First, you pay no postage. Second, you do not have to work hard to get potential customers to open them -- they're "in the face' of the prospect upon delivery. They are cheaper to print, and they take less time to read than full-length sales letters.

Distributing flyers can be done by children or teenagers -- or anyone looking to make a little extra money on a long afternoon. Even non-profit groups, such as the Boy Scouts or youth clubs looking to raise money can be enlisted to be your personal "flyer distribution army."

If you distribute your flyers in an area that has a need for what you are selling, response rates can easily be as high as 15%. When you consider direct mailers are ecstatic with 2% response, flyers look extremely attractive indeed.

Here is an interesting twist to help prevent your leaflet or pack being trashed if you are door dropping them.
Insert your leaflet or 'drop package' into a re-sealable plastic bag, with a letter urging them not to throw it away, as it will be recollected. This is particularly useful if you are dropping off a catalogue or response devise.

Flyers should be tested to determine how well they work. Fortunately, that is easy to do. Simply code your flyers by colour, with numbers, or with letters and then see which ones bring back the best results. Flyers will only work as well as the offer you make on them. Do not forget to use sizzling sales copy, a free offer, benefits, catchy headline, and easy contact info - and all the rest!

Fast Cash Tactics After Word...

Remember -- slow business and cash crunches happen! You would not be doing business right if they didn't.

The key is to find Tactics to bolster cash flow when you really need to. There is nothing worse than inaction.
When you think creatively, you can move out dead inventory, revitalize cash flow, and turn things around faster than you ever thought possible.

Losers see problems as problems. Winners see problems as opportunities. Dead inventory and stalled cash flow may be just the very thing you need to electrify your business!

XBS Module 3

Lead Generation

Getting an Endless Supply of High-Quality Leads for Your Business

Preparation is the key to your success and is the main reason why the XBS System Program is so successful

Introduction

Okay. You have discovered the 21 Business Building Principles and have already seen what you can do to quickly inject much needed cash and sales into your business.

Like we said earlier, the 'Quick Cash Tactics' should be an integral part of your overall marketing strategy. Do not just use them right now – keep using them. Why? Because they work. Only a fool stops using Tactics that are producing sales and profits for their business!

Now we are moving on to the start of putting your own XBS System in place. If you remember back to the

XBS System diagram on page 8, it shows the XBS KEYS.

What we are going to do now is show you how to maximise your results from each XBS KEY and explain what you need to do in precise step-by-step detail.

The first XBS KEY we are going to take you through is **LEAD GENERATION**.

Lead generation is something every business owner is aware of, but it is the least understood. Therefore, results are often poor – extremely poor.

The **foundation** of every successful business is preparation. And this is the single biggest reason why most business owners do not achieve the results they should. They do not prepare the business so it can quickly and easily generate the volume of high-quality leads necessary to expand and grow the business.

Therefore, your lead generation system has two main parts to it…

1. Preparation – Giving your business 'The WOW Factor' to make it easy to generate high quality leads (and as you will soon see – this is easy when you put in place all the steps required!).

2. Applying Proven Lead Generation Tools – As soon as you have done your preparation, you are ready to unleash a suite of powerful and proven lead generation tools.

Preparation is where we start…

Lead Generation – Preparation

Over the next several XBS Modules we will be showing you each component of 'Preparation,' that is crucial to making your business as successful as possible.

Here is what we will be preparing and putting in place…
- Niche Market(s)
- Creating Your Own USP (Unique Selling Proposition)
- Other Benefits of Your Product or Service
- Risk Reversal and Guarantees – Eliminating the Risk
- Creating Testimonials That Get Results
- Creating Irresistible Offers
- Choosing the Right Font to Make All Your Lead Generation Communications Easy To Read
- Lead Generation Strategy to Maximise Your Return on Investment
- Setting Your Objectives to Give You Direction
- 'Budgeting' For Your Lead Generation Marketing Tools Each preparation item will ensure two things when
- you start marketing your business…
- It will be easy to generate high quality leads
- And even easier to convert those leads into clients or customers.

Follow each preparation item step by step, and one after the other, and we promise you the rewards you seek. You will be surprised how easy all the other components of the XBS Program are to create.

It is vital that you follow each preparation item in sequence. They are in a logical and straightforward order.

We cannot emphasize enough how important the Preparation Modules are to you and your business. They will without doubt determine the scale of your success.

XBS Module 4

Niche Marketing

Multiply the size of your business by targeting specific people and businesses that have a perfect need for your product or service

Introduction

This first preparation item is the most important thing we will do together. No matter how amazing your product or service is. No matter how appealing your product or service is. And no matter how unique your product or service is – if you try to market and sell to the wrong people – you will very quickly go out of business.

Nothing is more certain than this!

What we are saying here is that you must define who your market is BEFORE you do anything else.

There is another crucial thing to mention about your market, and it is this…

Just accept this fact.

> **You can't be "all things to all men."**

So why do so many of us try to achieve this? In most cases it is because we're frightened to 'limit' the number of people we specifically target. We think if we reduce the number of prospects, we will risk our whole livelihood…

Nothing could be further from the truth. Here is why…

A common question we are often asked is this – "If I limit my market won't I be reducing the chances of doing business with more people?"

Of course, you will, but to succeed in today's competitive marketplace you need to concentrate your marketing on a smaller number of well-chosen segments or niches into which you pour all your resources.

> **A niche market is a specific group of people or businesses that want and need your product or service and can afford to pay for it!**

Because you are targeting smaller numbers, the same amount of money you were previously using to acquire clients or customers, is spread across a smaller number, and therefore you have more to spend on each prospect than you would if your market was bigger. This alone makes you more successful.

In a nutshell your niche market is the segment(s) that represents your best chance of getting a good return for your marketing efforts.

These niches are critical to you.

Of course, if you focus on a smaller group you may not get the business of other people or businesses outside the target group. However, what actually happens is you increase the amount of business you receive from your target group(s).

This is because you are specifically meeting your niche markets needs and requirements. You are saying to them that, 'you are THE company that knows about their situation.' No other company specifically meets their needs in this way, and therefore you are seen as the logical company to turn to.

Here is a simple but very powerful example of why defining your market or niche is so powerful…

Let us say you're a start-up business and you need an accountant. Your first choice is to look in the Yellow Pages under the 'Accountancy Category.' Although there are a number of ads.

The first one reads…

> 'ABC Chartered Accountants. Tax preparation, auditing, bookkeeping, payroll services, help for start-ups, management accounts, and so on'

The second ad reads…

> 'XYZ Chartered Accountants. Specializing in helping Start-Ups get their businesses running quickly, profitably and effectively.'

Which firm of accountants are you likely to choose?
The answer is obvious, but it serves a good example to show you how effective this strategy is — yet how widespread it is that few businesses follow this simple approach!

If you can create this bond between you and your niche market(s) we guarantee you will grow your business quicker than you could ever imagine.

Important Note:
The reason why this is THE first step in the XBS Program is because once you have decided who you are targeting, everything else follows. Your focus is your target market(s), and you build your whole XBS around these people.

That is why this Module is so important to you. What you will also discover is that once you have this focus everything else is easier to apply.

Make no mistake this is THE most important part of your whole business building system!

How to Choose Your Niche?

Now you know and understand why you need to define your target market or niche, let us see how you actually define the niche(s) that offers the maximum opportunity for your business.

There are 5 important stages you need to go through to select the perfect niche(s)…

Stage 1: Competitive Analysis

Stage 2: Your Own Company Analysis

Stage 3: Identifying Possible Niche(s)

Stage 4: Choosing Your Perfect Niche(s)

Stage 5: Define Your Chosen Niche(s)

Let us get started…

Stage 1: Competitive Analysis

If you were a general going into battle, we guarantee you would have studied your enemy or your adversary. You would look at previous battles won (and lost), how they won them (or lost them), what tactics they used, whether they used infantry or foot soldiers – or both, what weapons they used and so on.

You would want to build up a picture of them so you could counter any possible attack and focus on their weaknesses to hopefully win the battle.

Whether you like it or not, running a business is much like going to war. Okay your competitors should not be your enemies, but at the end of the day there can only be winners and losers. We want you not only to be a winner, but to be THE winner.

It goes without saying that because your prospects and clients or customers have to choose between you and your competitors, you must ensure you know who you're up against.

It staggers us that even though most people have a good idea who their competitors are – they rarely make the effort to analyze them thoroughly.

Much like the army general going into battle, if you know what your competitors are doing, you can defend against their strengths, and attack their weaknesses. The result when you get your marketing right (as of course you will, now you are a member of the 'XBS Program') is an overwhelming victory.

So why don't people study their competitors? As crazy as it seems, it is like everything – it takes time and effort, but the methods we're going to show right now will show you how to analyze your competitors very quickly and gain an unfair advantage over them.

What you are going to learn will help you instantly leapfrog any competitor – and that my friend will enable you to live your life as you choose!

Please Note:

At this point it's a good time for us to explain that whilst all our approaches are universal, there are sometimes slightly different techniques necessary, depending <u>not</u> on the product or service you sell, but whether you sell your product or service…

- **LOCALLY** (Product/Service Type 1)
- **REGIONALLY** (Product/Service Type 2)
- **NATIONALLY** (Product/Service Type 3)
- **WORLDWIDE** (Product/Service Type 4)

There are also a few occasions where we need to differentiate between…

New or recently established.

And

Established

If a different approach needs to be used during any XBS System Module, do not worry, we'll tell you and give you the exact steps you need to follow.

This is one case in point. Please use whichever method suits your circumstances best…

There are two simple methods for conducting competitor analysis for each of the four Product/Service Types above. Simply choose the category and then the method which suits you best…

Category 1: LOCALLY

Method 1: Your product or service type has a category in the Yellow Pages where 5 OR MORE of your competitors have display ads

The Yellow Pages is the perfect competitor analysis tool because it lists all your local competitors' side by side!

In this situation, we are defining a 'display ad' in the Yellow Pages as an ad that is at least 6.4cm high and 6.4cm wide. Smaller lineage, in-column ads, or semi-display ads do not count.

Here are the types of ads that **DON'T** qualify (please note depending on the country you reside in; the sizes will differ slightly) …

ABC Carpenters
Any Street, Any Town......... (012) 5678912   - One Line Listing (or In-Column ad)

ABC Carpenters Ltd
Any Street, Any Town, Any Post Code / Zip (01234) 56789

- 15 mm Semi-Display

Family run business with over 40 years' experience

Any Street, Any Town, Any Post Code / Zip   (01234) 56789

- 30mm Semi-Display

ABC Carpenters

- 45mm Semi-Display

Any ads **LARGER** than the previous one qualifies as display ads. In the UK, the following ad is the smallest display ad size: South Africa is similar

Family run business with over 40 year's experience

Any Street, Any Town, Any Post Code / Zip Car parking available

(01234) 56789

EMERGENY SERVICE

A B C
CARPENTETERS

This ¼ column display ad and ads larger than this are the ads you need to look at.

If there are 5 or more ads of this size or larger then you can use Method 1 for your competitor analysis

Please Note: These ads are shown to give you an idea on the size of ads you need to look at for your competitor analysis. They are certainly **NOT** given to show you how a great Yellow Pages ad looks like! More on this later!

If you're intrigued as to why we only want you to look at display ads it's simple… Display ads by their nature allow the advertiser to put more information in them, enabling you to assess your competition more quickly and effectively!

Here is what we want you to do…

STEP One

Create a spreadsheet or simply take a piece of paper and write the names of the competitors with display ads down the page/spreadsheet…

Here's an example (the category in this example is 'Personal Injury Lawyers') …

Firm/Company
Advance Legal
Ison Harrison & Co
Anderson Eden
Better
Freethcartwright Lawyers
The Claim Line
William Vaughan & P
Bray & Bray
A1 Accident Claims
Addison Yates Lawyers
1st Accident Claims
Accident Advice Helpline
Accident Line
Easy Claims
Proclaim
Ward & Rider
Accident Group
Ashley Ainsworth
Edwards Lawyers
Lawson-West
National Accident Helpline
PI Helpline
Rich & Carr
Shoosmiths
Fishers Lawyers

These are all the advertisers with display ads in the category (25 in this example)

STEP Two

Now look at each display ad and note down in the column next to the company names, if any of your competitors **target specific markets** or niches.

Do not just write 'yes' or 'no.' If they do mention a niche, write the name of the niche down. Even if they just mention the niche in the ad without focusing on it, you should write it down.

Here is what you should have (for ease we've just listed half a dozen companies from our previous example) …

Firm/Company	Niche
Advance Legal	RTA's (Road traffic accidents)
Ison Harrison & Co	No
Anderson Eden	Head Injuries
Better	No
Freethcartwright	No
The Claim Line	Women

STEP Three

Now add another column titled 'Focus.' Now you will note if the niche is focused or not.

For example, if we take the accountancy example from earlier…

Here is the first ad…

Ad 1: 'ABC Chartered Accountants. Tax preparation, auditing, bookkeeping, payroll services, help for start-ups, management accounts, and so one.'

…and the second ad…

Ad 2: 'XYZ Chartered Accountants. Specializing in helping Start-Ups get their businesses running quickly, profitably and effectively.'

Ad 1 mentions 'Start-Ups' but it does not **focus** on them. You would therefore enter 'no' in the Focus column.

Ad 2 completely focuses on 'Start-Ups' so in this example, you'd enter 'Yes' in the Focus column.

Here is what you should now have…

Firm/Company	Niche	Focus
Advance Legal	RTA's (Road traffic accidents)	Yes
Ison Harrison & Co	No	-
Anderson Eden	Head Injuries	No
Better	No	-
Freethcartwright	No	-
The Claim Line	Women	Yes

Please Note:

> You may now say, "well I know for a fact that so and so have a start-up section (or whatever) but I haven't noted it in my table."
>
> Here's why there's no need...
>
> If they don't mention their niche in their Yellow Pages ad — it's likely they don't communicate this well or even at all. So your prospects or clients or customers won't know they have specific niche(s).
>
> Only focus on what your competitors communicate — because that's all your prospects and clients or customers will focus on! Remember it's all about perception!

STEP Four

Having completed Steps 1-3 you should now know what target markets or niches your competitors are focusing on (if any!).

Keep this information to one side for now, we will be using it shortly.

Method 2: Your product or service type has a category in the Yellow Pages where LESS than 5 of your competitors have display ads.

If your category of the Yellow Pages does not have 5 or more display ads, then you need to use this method. Do not worry it's equally effective — but it takes a little longer!

STEP One

Still use the Yellow Pages, but this time you are going to ring each company listed (even if there are less than 5 display ads in your category, all your competitors will still be listed).

You may want someone else to do the phoning for you, but the purpose of the phone call is to get each competitor to send you some information about their product or service.

Here is what you'd say...

> "Hello I'm interested in your <Type of product or service> can you please send me some information before I take things further?"

If the competitor is interested. They may ask you some basic 'qualifying questions' (but this is highly unlikely). Just answer these always understanding that your sole objective is to get them to send you information.

If they try to make an appointment etc, just explain that before you do that you want to read about their product or service first.

Also ask if they have a web site — you may find all the information you need on their web site.

STEP Two

Once the information starts arriving your next task is to set up a simple spreadsheet or chart exactly how we did in Method 1 above.

You should be able to see if any of your competitors focus on any tested target markets or niches from the material, they send you.

Again, once you have completed this step, put the information to one side ready to use shortly.

Category 2: REGIONALLY

Method 1: Your product or service type has a category in the Yellow Pages where 5 OR MORE of your competitors have display ads

Apply all the steps listed above in Category 1: Method 1. The difference here is you would look at the ads across ALL the areas you operate in. That may mean you need to look in 5 or 6 (or more or less) different Yellow Pages books.

Remember if you operate regionally your competing against businesses across the region. That is why you need to look at the Yellow Pages books covering the entire area.

Method 2: Your product or service type has a category in the Yellow Pages where LESS than 5 of your competitors have display ads.

Apply the steps listed above in Category 1: Method 2. Once again, the difference here is to call each competitor that operates in your region.

Category 3: NATIONALLY

Method 1: Your product or service type has a category in the Yellow Pages where 5 OR MORE of your competitors have display ads

Again, apply the steps listed in Category 1: Method 1, only this time there is no need to look at every Yellow Page book. Just take a random selection (up to 12 books) in various parts of your country.

Remember, even though you may operate nationally, you are still competing with local businesses, that's why you need a good cross section of areas to analyze.

Method 2: Your product or service type has a category in the Yellow Pages where LESS than 5 of your competitors have display ads.

Apply the steps outlined in Category 1: Method 2, only this time take a random selection of areas and call no less than 50 businesses.

Yes, this takes time, but it is so important you can't skip this part!

Category 4: WORLDWIDE

Method 1: Your product or service type has a category in the Yellow Pages where 5 OR MORE of your competitors have display ads

Again, apply the steps listed in Category 1: Method 1, and then follow the same procedure as outlined above in the National Category Method 1 for each country you operate in.

You need to do this for each country because as you know there are differences in competition for each country.

Method 2: Your product or service type has a category in the Yellow Pages where LESS than 5 of your competitors have display ads.

Again, apply the steps listed in Category 1: Method 2, and then follow the same procedure as outlined above in the National Category Method 2 for each country you operate in.

Stage 2: Your Own Company Analysis

There are four situations that we need to take into account here…

1. **You Have No Idea at The Moment – You Need to Identify Your Niche(s)**

   You currently offer your product or service to 'everyone.' You need to find a niche(s) that you can focus on to rapidly grow your business.

2. **Uncovering Niches Already in Your Business**

   Often, you will find that you sell your product or service to one or more different client or customer types (niches) already. You just have to look at your client/customer list more carefully to uncover them.

3. **You already have a chosen niche, but you want to change because they are not profitable enough**

   Alternatively, you may be serving one or more niches already, but you want to change because these particular niches aren't profitable enough.

4. **You already have a chosen niche(s)**

   You may have a good idea of the types of clients or customers you serve well (but you need to confirm they are the best and most profitable to concentrate on), and you want to build your business around these already identified niche(s)

The following questions will help you identify potential target markets or niches…

1. What do you do well and enjoy at the same time?

   If you are offering more than one product or service, there may be one particular product or service you do better or enjoy more. If so, what types of people or businesses benefit from this product or service the most?

2. Which product(s) or service(s) do you offer that are the most profitable?

   If you offer more than one product or service, there will be certain ones that are more profitable than others.
   Once you know the answer to this, you can then ask yourself which types of people or businesses are these products or services most suitable for.

3. Who are your best clients or customers?

   Do 20% of your customers generate 80% of your profits?

   Find out who your best customers are (shame on you if you do not already know the answer to this!).

   What proportion of your profits do these top customers contribute to? What product or service are they buying? Is there a commonality?

4. Do your best clients have any similarities?

   If you sell your product or service to other businesses, what are the similarities? Look at the following indicators:

   - Industry Type
   - Turnover
   - Geographic Location

- Number of Employees
- The position or job title of the senior buyer for your services
- Number of offices or retail / distribution outlets

If you sell your product or service to consumers, what are their similarities? Look at the following indicators:

- Income
- Joint income
- Geographic Location
- Number of children
- Age
- Lifestyle habits and hobbies
- Employment type
- Their industry types
- What cars they drive

5. What is the profitability of each client or customer?

This is an especially important exercise for you to undertake. Look at all your customers and start analyzing them in terms of profit. What you will find is your customer list can be broken down or segmented into 2-5 different profit categories. It makes sense to focus on the most lucrative groups.

You need to look closely at the following…

- First order value
- Number of times (frequency) they buy your product or service
- Total revenue
- Costs to service the client or customer
- Total profit

Do not dismiss this as another 'hard and time-consuming job.' This one exercise alone is often very revealing (and often shocking) when you finally calculate the profit of each customer and customer group!

In many cases our clients have realized some groups are costing them money. If that is the case, you have three options…

The first thing to do is offer them an alternative more profitable product or service. If they do not 'upgrade' then apply one of the following…

- Write or phone them and tell them that due to the changes in the way you are operating your business you will not be able to service them any longer. In this case you would offer them an alternative provider of your product or service (see below for a better method)
- Speak to one of your competitors who you know offers the type of product or service these people are using. Then negotiate a fee based on you transferring your customers to them.

  Then all you would do is write to your customers recommending your competitor (just like an endorsed mailing). That way you earn money from your 'loss making' customers – and get rid of them at the same time!

6. Do your worst clients or customers have any similarities?

Go through the same process as you have just done for your best customers. Of course, avoid these groups like the plague!

7. Do you have any expertise relating to specific types of business or people?

You may find you have expertise in one or more areas that benefit certain types of people or businesses more

than others. For example, you may be a chartered accountant, but 'start up businesses' are your real area of expertise.

In this instance it would make sense to target new and startup businesses.

8. What did your competitor research reveal to you?

Having carried out your competitor research, you know who has specific niches and what they are. You also know how strong they are in these niches.

There are three areas you can look at to help you identify possible niches…

- Look at the niches that are not taken up by your competitors. If they are profitable add them to your list!

- If a niche is targeted by a competitor but they do not really focus on it – this represents a big opportunity for you. Write it down.

- Even if a competitor (or more than one competitor) is strong in a particular niche do not reject it. Depending on the size of the 'market' i.e. if the total number of potential customers (see below) is large, you can still be very wealthy by also choosing this market. Do not dismiss this niche until you've gone through the questions below (Making Sure Your Chosen Niche(s) Is PERFECT for You).

For New Businesses

Please Note:

If you have just started a new business you clearly won't have any customers to base most of this information on. So here's what to do (very similar to the exercise we took you through for the 'Competitor Analysis')…

- Look in the Yellow Pages under your business category. Look at what your competitors are doing – what they're not doing, and what appeals to you. Write all this information down.

- A good tip is to go to your local library and look at several different Yellow Pages directories in different locations to get even more information.

> If you're uncomfortable with this approach here's an alternative…
>
> Start with your friends and family.
>
> Are any of these people good potential prospects? We're almost certain at least a couple will be!
>
> What about asking your friends and family if they know of anyone who fits the description? They could mention to them what you're doing and ask them if they wouldn't mind helping you out by answering a few simple questions etc.
>
> Using this approach should give you at least 3 or 4 people to speak to without having to pick up the phone book.

- Now you should have a good understanding of what gaps and weaknesses (as well as the strengths) each of your competitors has.

- Next ring them up and ask them to send you information on the products or services they provide. You may want to ask friends to do this for you. This will give you even more detail.

- Finally ring up at least 6 potential prospects in each different niche that you are thinking about. Tell them that you are 'thinking' of setting up a new business and you'd really like to ask them a few questions.' Many people are only too happy to help. You must make it clear that you are **not** trying to sell them anything!

- Now you can find out what they want. What's missing from their current provider. What they like and dislike etc.

This approach should give you loads of ideas for deciding which specific niche(s) to focus on.

Stage 3: Identifying Possible Niches

Having answered all these questions, you should have identified one or more groups of people or businesses you can focus on.

If you have two or more groups, you feel you can serve well. Do not worry, that's okay.

Each different group represents one niche. If you have three groups, you have three niches and so on. The key is to communicate differently with each – and not to combine them all together!

But before you leap in the air, you need to make sure the group(s) you have identified are PERFECT for you…

Stage 4: Choosing The Perfect Niche

As you are now fully aware – customers are not all equal. So, having identified one or more niches, there are some critical questions you need to answer to be 100% certain that these groups are your ideal and most profitable choices...

1. What important need of this niche does your product or service fulfil?
2. What are the main needs, wants, problems, and frustrations of your niche? How does your product or service address each of these issues?
3. Do they have the money to pay for your product or service?
4. Will they pay a premium for a better product or service?
5. Where are they? Can you service them successfully in these geographic areas?
6. Are there many of them? How many in total? Depending on the product or service you sell, you will want to make sure there are enough of them to ensure your healthy existence! If the niche is too small, it really is not a niche!

Conversely if your niche is too big then it is not really a niche.

For example, 'providing career guidance to businesspeople' is too broad a definition for a focused niche, however the following examples would be excellent choices (notice the segments get more focused as we go down the list...

- Providing career advice to women in business
- Providing career advice to professional women
- Providing career advice to female Lawyers

A simple way to ascertain if your niche is big enough is to answer this simple question...

> 'Could your service business flourish if you won just 5% of the total market as clients or customers?'

If so, then great it passes the test. If not, you may have gone too specific and you need to widen the market or choose another (or additional) niche!

7. Is competition in this segment weak (or the market large enough for you to enter it)?

Here is where we'll use the research you've already carried out. You know the answer to this because of the competitor research you have already carried out.

8. Can your message be given to them easily?

This is massive. If your chosen niche cannot be reached easily and cost-effectively then drop them off your list.

Here is where they can be found easily…

- At home
- At work (what is their position in the company?)
- Meeting in their clubs and associations
- In the community
- Speak to a "list broker" to find out if these groups can be located on one or more mailing lists (99% of the time there will be a mailing list(s) available – no matter how obscure your niche may be!).

This is a particularly important part of your research. The good thing is that as long as you use a list broker – they'll do the work for you.

A list broker is just like an insurance broker. They are independent and have access to all the database lists on the market. Simply tell them what characteristics your niche market has, and they will go away and tell you which lists would be appropriate to use. You only pay when you decide to order the list!

Please take this advice on board. List brokers are a welcome addition to your "team" of suppliers. Even if you think your niche is diverse, do not think a list can't be found. You will be pleasantly surprised at the number of lists available!

To find any good list broker, simply look in your Yellow Pages under the category of 'Direct Mail.' Or do a search on the Internet using the keyword phrase, 'list broker.'

9. What publications do they read?

Often, your niche will read certain newspapers, magazines, trade journals etc. If so, they are easily reached through advertising. Do not worry. Using my proven advertising techniques will ensure your advertising becomes very profitable!).

10. Is the niche(s) a good match for you?
Use your instinct here. You may have chosen a niche that just does not fit well with you or your business. If so, strike it off your list.

11. Do you already have credibility with them?

This is not essential but it will give you a head start. Those niches where you have relevant experience and credibility are of course your best and quickest options.

After answering all these questions, you should be greatly confident in finally choosing one or more niches to focus on. But before you do, we want you to run each niche through the following 'Niche Rating Scale.'

You will notice there are 7 basic criteria that your niche must fulfil before you move confidently on. Simply score each criterion a mark out of 10 – with 10 being the absolute best score and 0 being the worst...

The Niche Market Rating Scale

My chosen niche wants the product or service I provide

My chosen niche can afford my product or service

My chosen niche will pay a premium for my product or service

I can reach my niche quickly, easily and cost- effectively

My chosen niche is large enough to make me wealthy

I have credibility with the chosen niche, or I can gain credibility quickly

The location of the chosen niche allows it to be serviced conveniently and cost-effectively

What you have done by rating each niche in this way is to determine your best niche(s) to focus on. Obviously, the higher the score the better the niche.

What to do if you only want to target one niche but two niches score the same?

Simple. Just ask yourself which niche you would enjoy working with the most!

Some Live Examples of Niche Markets...
- An accountant who focuses purely on start ups
- A portrait and wedding photographer whose niche are consumers who have a combined income of over R60,000
- A management consultant who targets furniture manufacturing companies employing over 100 people
- A training company that focuses on law firms with 4 or more partners
- A marketing consultant who focuses on service businesses with 5 – 50 employees
- A carpet cleaning company that targets families living in detached homes with 3-6 bedrooms in a 50-mile radius of their office
- A manufacturer of printing devices selling to two niches – printers and print finishers in the UK

Next, we will define your chosen niche(s)...

Stage 5: Defining Your Chosen Niche

Now that you have chosen one or more niches you need to clarify the exact characteristics of each niche. This ensures you only focus on your ideal clients or customers, and as a result makes you more profitable and more successful than you ever thought possible!

What we will be doing is creating the perfect 'profile' of your niche(s). The good news is you will have uncovered all of these characteristics already during this XBS Module.

Here is what to include if you're niche is a business segment...
- The specific type of industry or portion of the industry

- The company size (by turnover, profit, employees etc)

- The job title (and the titles of other people who may influence the sale)
- Geographic location
- The biggest problem they want to solve and how you solve it
- The product(s) or service(s) they will be buying from you

Here is what to include if your niche is a consumer segment...
- The person (male or female) that makes the decisions or is it a joint decision
- Their income, size of house, number of cars, children, married, etc
- Geographic location
- The biggest problem they want to solve and how you solve it
- The service they will be buying from you

Well done. You have now created the **perfect** 'Niche Business.' We guarantee if you follow these **simple** steps, you will start seeing a huge return on your time and effort.

Now we are moving on to the next preparation item – Unique Selling Proposition...

XBS Module 5

Unique Selling Proposition

The second most important thing you must do to grow your business is to construct your own "Unique Selling Proposition" – get this right and your targeted prospects (your niche) will not be able to resist your product or service!

Introduction

What would be your answer to this question…? "What's the one unique thing you offer that makes your prospects think – wow, I must have this product or service?"

If you are like 99% of people running a business your answer will be at best – very vague. Few people spend the time to articulate what it is they do that is so unique and special for the client or customer.

If you cannot accurately describe this uniqueness to your prospects, what chance have they got to find out what you offer – over and above your Competitors?

USP is the one real benefit that differentiates you from your competition in the mind of your prospect. It is all about what the prospect receives – what result they get from you – what it is that's going to make a positive difference to their life.

If your prospect can immediately see what it is, you do that is so unique and they find it irresistible – you have created the **perfect** USP.

One more point to add. You can have a unique benefit that may not actually be unique, as long as it is **PERCEIVED** to be unique. Let us explain…

Very few companies communicate their uniqueness. Therefore, even if one of your competitors offers what you offer, the chances are, they do not tell anyone about it.
Therefore, as far as your prospect or client is concerned this **IS** unique.

To help you understand this further we'll tell you a classic story that dates back to the 1920's in the USA…

A beer company called Schlitz Beer was at the time an unsuccessful brewing company lying a lowly 8th in their market. They went to **number 1** in six short months by using a perceived USP that was not unique.

Here is what happened…

During this time there were eight or nine different brewing companies aggressively competing for the same market. Everyone was

communicating the same message that their
beer was the purest. They did not explain what pure meant to the beer drinker, they just kept saying that it was pure, pure, pure.
Unfortunately for Schlitz they were losing ground.

Luckily for them they were introduced to Claude Hopkins - one of true greats of marketing. Many of his Tactics are still being used today by people like me. Claude asked to be taken around their manufacturing plant.

Like all good marketing people, he wanted as much background information as possible.

As he was being shown around the Schlitz plant, he was amazed at how they made their beer.

First and foremost, their facilities were right on the base of Lake Michigan. Back in the early twenties this water was very pure. Despite this, Schlitz sunk two 5,000-feet deep artesian wells on the shores because they had to go deep enough to find the right combination of water with the mineral content to make the best possible beer.

They explained how they went through 1623 different tests and experiments over 5 years to identify the finest mother yeast cell that could produce the richest taste and flavor. They showed him the intricate process of distillation of the water where it was heated to 5,000 degrees F, and then cooled down and condensed. They carried out this process three times to ensure the water was absolutely purified.

They talked about the bottling process where they steamed each bottle at temperatures of 1600 degrees F to kill all bacteria. They finished by telling Claude they had every batch tasted to make sure it was indeed pure and rich before they would even bottle it and sent it out the door.

Claude was staggered. The lengths Schlitz went through to purify their beer was amazing. He said to them, "Why don't you tell people this story?" They replied by saying, "Everybody goes through this process, it's not unique – it's what must be done to ensure the beer is so pure."

> Claude replied by saying, "No one knows about this. The first person who tells this story will gain distinction and pre-eminence in their marketplace from then on."
>
> Schlitz was the first and only beer company that ever told the story of how their beer was formed. It made the word "pure" take on a totally different meaning in the eyes of their prospects and customers.

The impact was instant and remarkable. A rise to number 1 from number 8 in just six short months. That is the power of USP and perceived USP!

USP really is one of the most powerful concepts you can apply to your business! The good news is that it is actually quite simple to create!

So how do you create your USP?

There are several simple stages you will need to go through before being able to articulate your USP. Here is what we'll be covering together…

Step 1: Understand that you are not selling a product or service, you're selling a major solution to your niche's most pressing problem(s).

List the problems faced by your specific niche(s) and explain HOW you solve them

Step 2: In an ideal world what would your chosen niche(s) want from your type of product or service?

Step 3: Defining your USP - The two simple elements of USP

Step 4: Refining your USP

Step 5: Testing

Step 6: Refine (if necessary)

Step 7: Using your USP

Let us now take each step one at a time…

Step 1: Understand that you are not selling a product or service, you're selling a major solution to your niche's most pressing problem(s).

Think about the following situation…

You are out for a business lunch and someone who you've been speaking to asks you this very familiar question…

> **"What do you do for a living?"**

Now if you are a Lawyer or a printer we're almost certain you'll answer in this way…

"I'm a Lawyer"

"I'm a printer"

These are quite common replies and explain why most people 'switch off' after asking this question.

What you must realize is that when you answer in this way, you are saying what you ARE, rather than what you DO FOR YOUR CLIENTS OR CUSTOMERS! There's a massive difference.

The good news is this…

All your competitors answer in this way. All your competitors do not have a USP. All your competitors are selling is the 'product' or the 'service' and not the result!

To show you what we mean let us take the two examples above and add a USP…

> Lawyer – "I help people separate within 12 weeks and as amicably as possible"
>
> Printer – "I help people sell more of their products or services using innovative and cost-effective printed materials"

In essence your USP completely focuses on what you do for your specific niche(s). It is **the** major benefit.

By focusing on your clients or customers most pressing problems you can uncover your major benefit.

Think about your prospects and clients fears, obstacles and problems. How does your product or service reduce or eliminate these fears? For example, a telemarketing service company would say the major problem their prospects and clients have is…

They cannot generate enough leads or enquiries themselves

Here is how you'd then turn this problem into a powerful benefit…

Problem: They cannot generate any leads or enquiries **Benefit:** We help businesses generate high quality leads Do you see how easy this is?

So, having identified the major problem your product or service solves for your chosen niche(s), write the corresponding benefit down.

That is one powerful way of creating your USP. But do not stop there. We need to first explore another very profitable method…

Step 2: In an ideal world what would your chosen niche(s) want from your type of product or service

Some of the greatest businesses in the world were founded on such thinking...

Fed Ex (next day delivery guaranteed), Microsoft (to make the computer accessible and easy to use for everyone), Domino's Pizza (red hot pizza delivered to your door in less than 30 minutes).

Can you inexpensively reposition your basic offer to meet your clients or customers major need?

If so, write it down using the benefit approach we used in Step 1.

Step 3: Defining your USP - The two simple elements of USP

You should now be left with a fairly short list of options. That is okay. Now we need to start adding power to your USP. Once you have gone through this stage, if you have two or more options, you'll quickly be able to determine which USP really stands out.

Here are the two simple elements of USP...

1. **Focus the Opening On Your Niche And Combine With An Action Word:**

The first part of your USP tells what you do and WHO you do it for. The 'who' is of course your chosen niche(s).

This is where it starts to get exciting. And this is the first time you will understand why we started the 'XBS Program' with niche markets.

> **Please Note:**
> If you've chosen two or more niches that's okay, but you need to create a specific USP for each niche!

The key is to use a powerful action word with your niche to make the opening powerful.

For example, action words that work well are:

help, show, support, etc.

So here are some examples of openings using this simple approach (we are using the examples earlier for a Lawyer, and a printer – notice these previous examples didn't tie into a niche. We did this purposely so you can see the massive effect you get when you tie your USP into your chosen niche) ...

Lawyer:

> "I help people..."

Lawyer now focusing on the chosen niche...

> "I help unhappy couples..."

Printer:

> "I help people..."

Printer now focusing on the chosen niche...

> "I help small local businesses..."

2. Add The Major Benefit

The second (and final part) of your USP provides the solution to your chosen niche(s) most pressing problem or major need.

You have already created this part of your benefit statement, so simply add it to the opening. Here is what we've got with the examples above…

Lawyer:

> **"I help unhappy couples separate quickly and as amicably as possible"**

Printer:

> **"I help small local businesses sell more of their products or services using innovative and cost-effective printed materials"**

Can you see how effective your USP is? Just one sentence is all it takes, and you have elevated yourself above all your competition!

But you are not quite finished yet, even though you deserve a big pat on the back!

Step 4: Refining your USP

What we suggest you do now is sleep on it. Give yourself 24 hours before you come back to your USP. You will find you may be able to take out or change a word or two to make it punchier and more powerful.

Look for jargon words that few people understand and replace with a simple alternative. Your USP should be clear and easy to understand!

Step 5: Testing

Next try it out on yourself. Be impartial – does your USP make you think – 'WOW I want that!' if not we suggest you have got some more work to do.

Once you are happy with it go and show a couple of your clients or customers (if you haven't got any clients or customers, just ask friends who have a need for your product or service. Ask them to be honest!).

Step 6: Refine (if necessary)

If changes need to be made make them and then repeat Step 5 until you are completely happy with your USP.

Step 7: Using your USP

Having spent all this time creating your USP you now need to make sure your clients or customers and particularly your prospects know about it (remember although your USP benefits your clients – we are concentrating on lead generation here). This is critical!

If your clients or customers and prospects do not know about your USP there's no point in having one!

So how do you maximise the effectiveness of your USP? …

- Keep your USP written down and read it every day. Memorize it and use it in conversation with other people. When people ask, 'What do you do?' remember you must reply with your USP and NOT tell them what you are (an accountant, a management consultant, a printer etc).

- Use it in any other written communication to prospects.

- Use your USP as the headline in any of your lead generation tools (such as sales letters, ads etc).

- It is important you apply your USP to everything you're doing right now, because it will have an instant impact on your business. Of course, you will be using it from now on in almost every XBS System Module we'll be covering together over the coming days and weeks and Months, but we don't want you to wait.

Well done!

Your USP will help you transform your business. We do not say this lightly. Your USP can take you from an ordinary company to an extraordinary company in a few short months!

Keep using and developing your USP and your results will improve week by week!

XBS Module 6

Transferring The Features Of Your Product Or Service Into Sizzling Benefits

The benefits you provide are important to your prospects and clients or customers – benefits are what they are buying

Introduction

Okay now you have got a highly polished USP. That is great. We have installed the first stage of the 'WOW Factor' into your business. Now we need to build on this and write down the other benefits you provide for your clients or customers.

Remember people do not in reality buy your product or service and what you do for them (features), they buy the results your product or service brings them (benefits).

This is an amazingly simple approach. 95% of all businesses DON'T convert the features of their product or service into benefits. This results in fewer leads and less sales. That means the moment you start communicating your benefits – you will get more leads and more sales. Nothing is more certain.

The good news is that it is easy to take any of your features (no matter how mundane they may seem to you) and bring them alive in the minds of your potential clients or customers.

But first let us take a look at the Stages involved…

- **Stage 1:** What benefits are your competitors offering?
- **Stage 2:** Build your list of benefits to completely surpass any of your competitors using our principle of 'Benefit Pile-Up.' This alone will make you irresistible to your potential clients or customers!

Let us move on…

Stage 1: What benefits are your competitors offering?

This is such a great and sneaky technique you will wonder why no-one else does it! What you are going to do is create a list of benefits, built up from a combination of all your competitors.

Actually, what you're really doing is listing the features of what your competitors are offering – because most of your competitors will only list the features. But that is okay.
Stage 2 looks at how you convert these features into benefits.

This exercise is especially important for four reasons…
1. It gives you the entire list of features and benefits your competitors are offering. That is important because your potential clients or customers are buying these benefits (not the product or service itself)
2. It means you are not starting from a blank sheet, which is always more difficult
3. It will show you how poor your competitors are at selling benefits rather than features. Once you convert your features into benefits, you will have a huge competitive advantage
4. It will ultimately demonstrate how amazing our principle of Benefit Pile-Up really is!
5. So, let us move on…

- **STEP One**

Go back to the earlier section on 'Niche Markets.' Remember you created a list of your competitors during the 'Competitive Analysis stage of defining your Niche(s).'

We are going to work with this **same** list again today.

Take your spreadsheet and list the names of your competitors down the first column.

We are again using my working example of a firm of Lawyers to show you how this looks (see next page).

Firm/Competitor
1st Accident Claims
A1 Accident Claims
Accident Advice
Accident Group
Accident Line
Addison Yates
Advance Legal
Anderson Eden
Ashley Ainsworth
Better
Bray & Bray
Easy Claims
Edwards Solicitors
Fishers Solicitors
Freethcartwright
Ison Harrison & Co
Lawson-West
National Accident
PI Helpline
Proclaim
Rich & Carr
Shoosmiths
The Claim Line
Ward & Rider
William Vaughan

- **STEP Two**

In the next columns to the right of your competitors, you're going to add all the 'features/benefits' of the products or services provided by all these competitors.

This will instantly give you a great overall picture of the benefits provided by each competitor.

Here is how your spreadsheet should now look

Firm/Competitor	Features/Benefits																		
	Fee Free	No Win No Fee	No Win No Cost	100% Of Damages	Freephone	Local Office	Specialization	No Risk Claim	Free Home Visits	Specialist PI Lawyer	Law Society End.	Free Physiotherapist	No Loans	No Insurance	No Disbursements	No Doctors Fees	Guaranteed Damages	Solicitor 48 hours	Free Advice	Chq For R500	Testimonials
1st Accident Claims					1				1	1											
A1 Accident Claims	1			1	1																
Accident Advice	1									1											
Accident Group	1				1																
Accident Line	1				1						1										

Company																				
Addison Yates				1		1	1	1												
Advance Legal	1	1		1	1	1			1			1	1	1	1					
Anderson Eden		1			1	1		1	1							1				
Ashley Ainsworth		1			1															
Better		1			1			1	1	1										
Bray & Bray		1				1		1	1											
Easy Claims		1			1													1		
Edwards Solicitors					1															
Fishers Solicitors					1															
Freethcartwright		1			1			1	1											
Ison Harrison & Co		1		1	1			1	1											
Lawson-West					1															
National Accident				1	1															
PI Helpline		1		1																
Proclaim		1	1	1																
Rich & Carr					1															
Shoosmiths				1																
The Claim Line	1		1	1	1				1											
Ward & Rider		1		1	1															
William Vaughan		1			1		1	1												

Notice we have placed a '1' in the columns to signify the feature/benefit each company offers.

> **Please Note:**
>
> You'll see we've included a column on the far right of this spreadsheet titled, 'Testimonials.' Although this isn't necessarily a 'benefit' you should include this column to signify how many of your competitors use testimonials in their marketing.

> When you consider the incredible selling power of testimonials, you'll be surprised to see how few of your competitors are using them. We'll shortly be showing you how easy it is to get great testimonials!

- **STEP Three**

    Next total up the features/benefits for each competitor and add the total in the last column. Once you have done that, sort the order of competitors from the highest number of features listed to the lowest.

    Here is what this looks like...

			Features																	
Advance Legal	RTA's	Yes	1	1		1	1						1	1	1	1				
Ison Harrison & Co	No	-		1		1			1											
Anderson Eden	Head Injuries	No		1		1			1						1					
Better	No	-		1		1			1		1									
Bray & Bray	No	-		1					1											
Freethcartwright	No	-		1					1											
The Claim Line	Women	Yes	1			1	1													
William Vaughan	No	-		1					1											
A1 Accident Claims	No	-		1		1														
Addison Yates	No	-				1		1	1											
1st Accident Claims	No	-				1			1											
Accident Advice	No	-		1																
Accident Line	No	-		1		1					1									
Easy Claims	No	-		1		1											1			
Proclaim	No	-		1	1	1														
Ward & Rider	No	-		1		1														
Accident Group	No	-		1		1														
Ashley Ainsworth	No	-		1		1														
Edwards Solicitors	No	-																		
Lawson-West	No	-																		
National Accident	No	-				1														
PI Helpline	No	-		1		1														
Rich & Carr	No	-																		
Shoesmith	NO	-	1																	

Once you have finished this simple exercise, there are several things you'll be able to see...

- Only in an extraordinary case will any one competitor communicate every feature/benefit (we have never seen it!)

- Only in extraordinary circumstances will any competitor convert all the features into benefits (we have never seen it!)

- You will be able to see (once you've completed Stage 2), what features/benefits your competitors are missing! That spells 'Big Opportunity' for you!
- You will be able to reduce this total list by eliminating meaningless (weak and not worth communicating) and very similar features/benefits.
- For instance, in our working example above we would eliminate the following…
- *Free Fee (means the same as no-win no fee)*
- *No Risk Claim (means the same as no-win, no fee)*
- You will instantly see which competitors are better at marketing than others. Often this translates into 'more successful,' which means they are your biggest competitors!
- You can instantly gain massive competitive advantage when you communicate **all** the 'relevant' features/benefits (see below).

Stage 2: Build your list of benefits to completely surpass any of your competitors using our principle of 'Benefit Pile-Up.' This alone will make you irresistible to your potential clients or customers (niche)!

Now we're going to take all the relevant features and benefits you discovered above, and combine them with your own features and benefits to give you such an advantage your potential clients or customers (niche) will be compelled to choose you!

Here is what to do…

- **Step One**

First, we want you to list the features of **your** product(s) or service(s) and the corresponding benefits.

The best way to do this is to get a piece of paper, draw a line down the middle and write 'Features' on the left side and 'Benefits' on the right side.

First let us take a simple 'product' to show you how easy this is.

Here are 4 features and the corresponding benefits of a desk top hole punch (if we can get four benefits out of a very basic inanimate object you should be able to get at least the same amount for your product or service!)…

Feature	Benefit
Hole punch is made of hardened steel	It will last forever. You will never have to buy another one as long as you live.
The base has a plastic cover	The base collects all the punched-out paper, which ensures your desk stays clean no matter how often the punch is used.
The base is removable	Once the punch is full you simply clip off the base and place the excess waste into your bin. Easy to empty and it leaves no mess.
The punch has a plastic guide for your paper	Simply adjust the sturdy guide to the size of paper you want to punch. You get perfect results every time.

Here is a similar exercise for an accountancy practice…

Feature	Benefit
Free advice line	You can get proven business advice without paying for it!
A selection of services	You choose the services that suit your specific circumstances – therefore you only pay for what you need and want. There is no waste!
Open late on Wednesday's	Come and see us after work for no extra charge. Perfect if you are very busy or you just can't get out of the office through the day. We make it easy for you!

Do you see how easy this is?

> **Please Note:**
>
> To make this exercise easier you may want to write the following words after the feature — 'which means that.' These 3 words help connect the feature to the benefit making it easier to find the most powerful benefit.
>
> Plus as you compile your own list, make sure your benefits are related to the chosen niche(s) you selected earlier.
>
> This instantly adds selling power and persuasion to everything you do!

- **Step Two**

Now cross-reference all the features and benefits you provide with the list you compiled in Stage 1 above.

Now you will see some glaring gaps and some great additions.

- **Step Three**

Take all the features and benefits on your competitors list you have not included in your own list and ask yourself; can I include them?

You will find that in most cases you can easily add these features/benefits without changing the way you run your business.

Do not worry about being able to include everything. You will still be leaps and bounds ahead of your nearest competitor!

- **Step Four**

Now for the features/benefits you have added to your list (taken from the competitors list) make sure you convert the features into benefits just like you did for your initial list (in Step One above).

- **Step Five**

Add your features/benefits up and make sure they total **more** than the highest competitor. If they do not, you'll need to do some more thinking or include other features/benefits you originally discounted from the competitors list.

- **Step Six**

Now arrange your list **in order of importance**. So, your top benefit is the most important benefit. Remember this is a list based on what your clients or customers think are most important.

If you do not know yourself, simply ask a small selection of your clients or customers what order they'd put the benefits!

- **Step Seven**

Now you have your 'Benefit Pile-Up' list. This is a list of benefits you provide in order of importance (to the client/customer). You will be communicating this list in everything you do from now on – in ads, letters, your web site etc!

Often the best way to do this (and we suggest you adopt this simple approach), is to list your benefits as a series of bullet points.

Let us show you how this is done by taking our earlier Lawyer example…

The FREE Walk-In Advice Service…

Speed: We guarantee you will be spoken to by one of our serious injury specialist lawyers <u>within 10 minutes</u>

Flexibility: Speak to one of our specialist lawyers at <u>ANY time</u> Monday-Friday 9am – 6pm

Free Specialist Advice: Your conversation with one of our lawyers is <u>free no matter how long it takes</u>.

Concrete Advice and a Result: At the end of the conversation we will tell you if we think you have a good chance of <u>success</u> or not

Other Important Benefits…

Local Service: All our lawyers live in Leicestershire. That is why we can offer a truly <u>personal</u> and caring local service

Absolutely No Risk: No win, no fee – guaranteed.

100% Damages: You get 100% of the damages (subject to funding)

Free Visits: Once your case is underway, we will visit you at home, at work, or in hospital. Of course, we can also meet at our offices

Specialist Personal Injury Lawyers: Only specialist, fully qualified, and experienced lawyers will deal with your case from start to finish

Very High Success Rate: In the last year alone, we have won over R4.5 million in damages for our clients in Leicestershire. 80% of this was for serious injury claims!

Quick Progress Guaranteed: Our unique service approach ensures your case gets moving very quickly (10 weeks is our current record from starting a case to winning damages for the client)

Financial Help: Interim compensation may be available to assist your financial situation

Caring But Firm Approach: We are friendly and sympathetic, but very determined to win your case and get you every cent you deserve!

You should study how we have created this list of benefits. Notice how we have separated what we considered to be the most important benefit (USP) from the rest of the benefits.

If you look at the earlier list of features/benefits for this example, you will see that even though it's a well-known fact that other firms offer **'free advice'** they didn't communicate this. In fact, just 4 firms communicated this benefit. We made this element totally unique by calling it a 'FREE Walk-In Advice Service.'

Yes, that is a small change, but the results have been startling. You can take anything like this and put a different slant on it – and hey presto you have created something that your potential clients or customers can't resist!

Do you now see the power of 'Benefit Pile-Up'?

Since you have gone through this simple exercise you now know that your product or service offers the greatest level of benefits to your potential clients or customers (niche).

This is a massive advantage. It is only a matter of time before your leads and sales start multiplying! Well done!

XBS Module 7

Module 7 Risk Reversal

One of the few marketing tools you can use instantly to multiply the size of your business overnight!

Introduction

Listen to us carefully. If you put in place a powerful risk reversal (guarantee) tomorrow, you will be staggered by the success it achieves for you in the coming days, weeks, months and years.

As you know, the benefit of your product or service is gained after the sale is made. Sometimes this can be days, weeks, months or even years after the first sale was made. This in itself places an enormous risk on the shoulders of would be clients or customers. It is this risk that often prevents them from buying.

However, if you lower or eliminate the risk, then the natural consequence is people will be more inclined to buy from you.

That is the secret of creating a powerful risk reversal.

Your risk reversal is nothing more than a simple method that takes the 'barriers' away from the prospect, and ensures their objections and worries are taken away making it easy from them to buy from you.

To show you how this strategy works please see the diagrams on the next page…

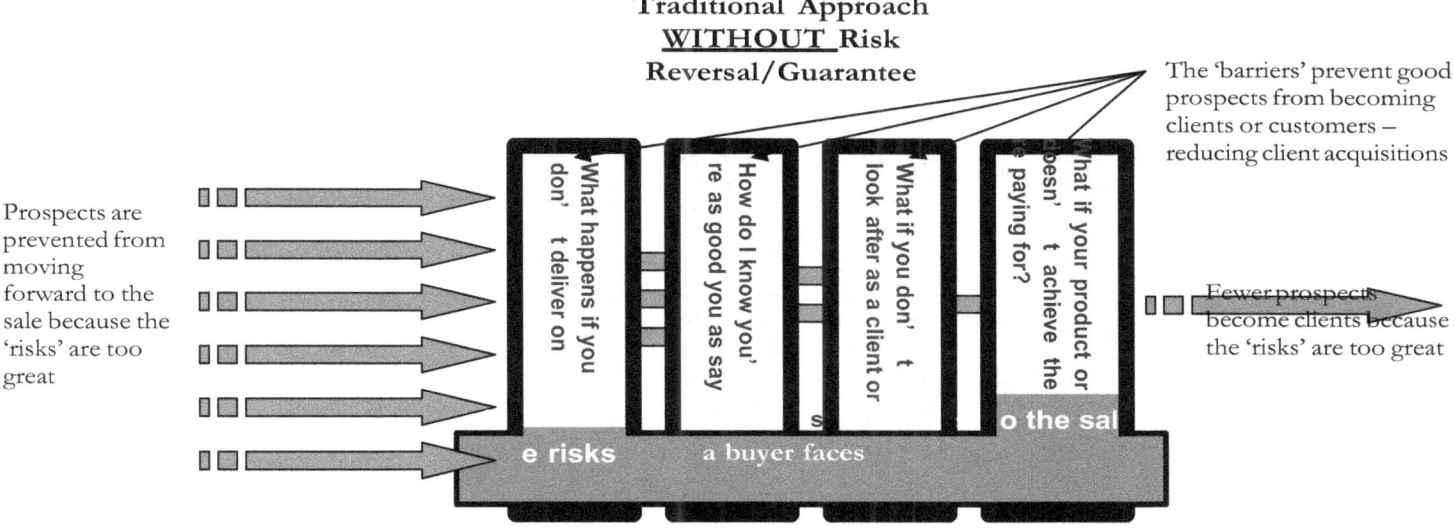

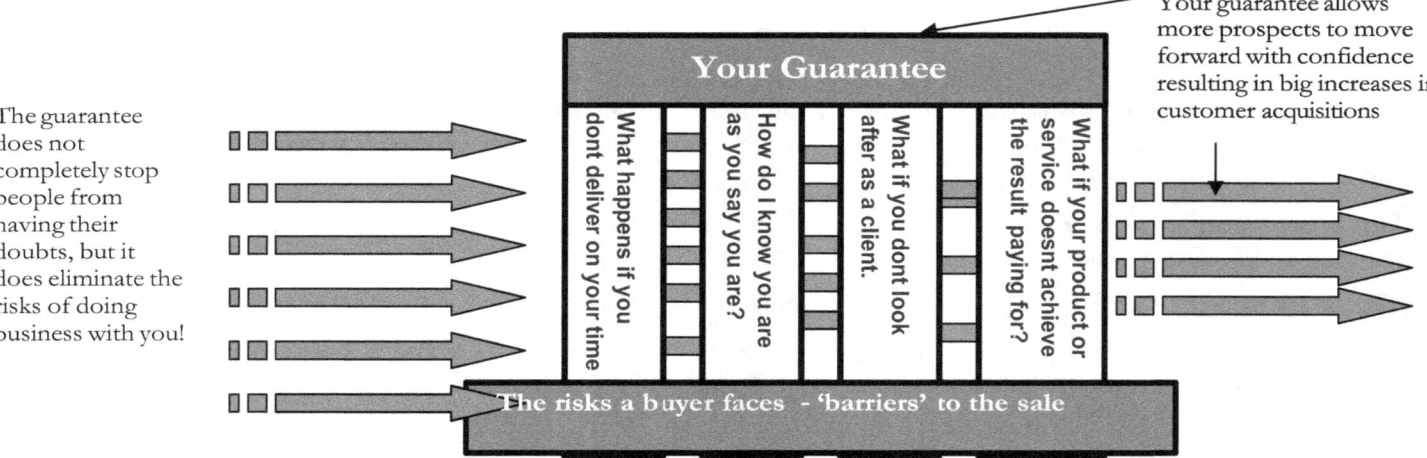

As soon as you add a guarantee to your business you...
- Remove the risks gaining more clients or customers
- Automatically differentiate your business from your competition
- And, your prospects will value your business much more, because they will automatically assume you must be excellent at delivering your product or service (why would you offer a guarantee if your service or your product wasn't great?)

The result is BIG increase in sales and an avalanche of clients or customers!

The ultimate is to guarantee the result of your product or service and add a 'penalty' should you fail. Here is how it looks...

Perfect Guarantee

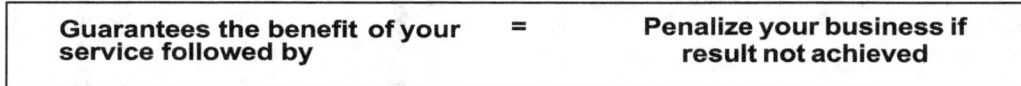

Please do not dismiss this. This one principle can grow your business overnight.

But before we move on let us take a closer look at Risk Reversal, so we can explain further what risk reversal is all about?

First let us ask you this simple question...

1. Do you stand behind what you do?

Of course, you do. And this is the **key** to risk reversal!

In **every** business transaction there is a **risk** involved. 99% of the time it is the person or business who <u>buys</u> your product or service who takes on this risk.

Do not forget one of the main problems you have (everyone has this problem) is that your clients or customers only benefit from your product or service <u>after</u> they've bought it. This risk is what prevents many people from buying.

Therefore, if you lower or eliminate the risk (the barriers shown above), your sales will multiply - literally overnight.

The concept is simple. As long as you provide a good product or service (it doesn't have to be great) to your clients or customers, then risk reversal will draw prospects to you like a magnet – and be a massive help for you when converting your leads into sales.

> **Please Note:**
> Risk reversal is essentially a 'sales conversion strategy' but it's so powerful it is also a very effective part of your lead generation. That's why we've included it as part of your lead generation preparation!

Here is a simple example of how risk reversal works:

A man wants to buy a puppy for his daughter. He responds to two ads in the local newsagent window. He examines the first puppy, and it seems ideal in temperament, and looks. The man says to him, "If the dog isn't right for your daughter, bring it back in one week and I'll give you your money back."

Clearly, he appreciated the value of risk reversal, but he did not fully understand it!

<u>The man then goes to look at the second puppy…</u>

Again, it seems ideal in temperament, and looks. Only this time the owner says, "Your daughter is obviously looking forward to her new puppy and it's important that she's totally happy with it. Please take the puppy, let your daughter play with it, look after it, and get to know it. If after three weeks the puppy is perfect for her, pay me for it. If not, just bring it back and owe me nothing!"

Now this man really understands risk reversal. First, he extended the "trial" period. He knows that his puppy is a good dog. He also knows after three weeks the puppy and girl will be inseparable. He totally reverses the risk.

You also need to understand this…

The company that reverses the risk, **automatically** gains competitive **advantage,** and wins more business – in fact much more! This competitive advantage is incredibly significant when attracting new clients to your service business.

> **Please Note:**
> Since risk reversal is so powerful, once you've defined your own risk reversal you may want to incorporate it into your USP (Unique Perceived Benefit). It will add considerable power to your USP.

We saw the following risk reversal when we went to the United States a few years ago. It is one of the **best** we've ever seen. It is from a pest control company called BBBK. Their guarantee is aimed at hotels and restaurants (their niches):

> "You don't owe one cent until all the pests on your premises have been eradicated...if you are ever dissatisfied with BBBK's services you will receive a refund for up to 12 months of the company's services...plus fees for another exterminator of your choice for the next year.
>
> If a guest spots a pest on your premises, BBBK will pay for the guests meal or room, send a letter of apology, and pay for a future meal or stay...and if your facility is closed down due to the presence of roaches or rodents, BBBK will pay any fines, as well as all lost profits, plus R5,000."

Although we do not know for certain, it's easy to **assume** several things about BBBK from this guarantee:

- They are particularly good at pest control.
- They understand the concerns of their clients with regard to hygiene.
- They are extraordinarily successful at attracting new clients!
- They are probably providing remarkably similar services as their competitors. However, they understand risk reversal and their **profits** we are sure will reflect this!

Okay. Hopefully, you now have a basic grasp of risk reversal and what it can achieve for your business. If you have given any thought to the strategy one question may be entering your mind...

"What about people taking advantage of my Risk Reversal, won't people try to abuse what I'm offering?"

The key of course to successful risk reversal is this – if you offer a quality product or service (in today's standards your product or service just needs to be half-decent, and you'll wipe the floor!) then you have nothing to worry about.

Unfortunately, we cannot say no one will ask for a refund or for their money back (or whatever your risk reversal states). What we can say is that for every one of these, you will attract many, many more prospects and clients or customers by simply offering a risk reversal in the first place.

Do not worry about this. Your risk reversal strategy is usually the one thing that tips the scales in your favor. Because you offer risk reversal, your prospect thinks and assumes the following things about you...

- If you are offering this risk reversal guarantee, you must be very good at what you do
- You must be 'stupid' to offer such a guarantee if you were poor at delivering your promises
- In the prospect's mind your risk reversal has 'proven' to him or her that you can give them exactly what they need.
- More importantly, when most people choose to buy a product or service, they choose it for perfectly **good reasons** and intentions. And they spend time making their decision.

- They would not choose you in the first place if they wanted to capitalize on your risk reversal.

The best way to stir your imagination (before we show you how to create your own risk reversal) is to show you some real-life proven risk reversal Tactics our clients and customers use...

Live Examples of Risk Reversal Property Management

Try us FREE for six months (180 days). During this time, we'll carry out all the property management tasks necessary for the smooth running of your property portfolio. If after this time you <u>don't</u> think we're managing your properties better than anyone before and we don't meet your high expectations, then you can simply stop the arrangement at absolutely no charge to you or your company.

Management Consultant

<u>Our Guarantee to You</u>

1. After the first month you can terminate our arrangement at any time if you are unhappy with the work we do. You just pay us for the work we've done.
2. If after the first 12 months following the completion of an assignment, you haven't had a return of at least 150% on your investment, we'll return all the fees you've paid.

Network Organisation

Guaranteed 500% return on your investment within the first 12 months or we'll:

Refund your whole membership fees

AND...

Allow you to keep the first year Go M.A.D videos worth R885.00, and the 12 months of audio tapes worth R130.00

AND...

We'll give you the fourth Go M.A.D video worth R295.00 just for your trouble

Computer Software Training

Train with us for two hours. If you don't think the training is of great benefit to you then you can say so and walk away. We'll refund your money immediately - no questions asked.

Message Taking Service

Try our telephone answering service FREE for 30 days without any cost or obligation. If after 30 days you're not totally satisfied, we'll cancel the service, and you'll owe us nothing!

Structural Engineer
1. FREE preliminary structural consultation undertaken at your office.
2. FREE quotation for structural engineering services.
3. No job - no fee!

Telemarketing / Lead Generation <u>**Generating You Sales Leads For Just R65 Each**</u>

You only pay for the sales leads we generate. You don't pay us a single cent for unsuccessful calls. If we generate 10 quality sales leads for you, all you pay us is R650. If it took us 100 or 1000 calls to generate these leads for you it doesn't matter you still pay us just R650 – interested?

Software Training – Blue Chip Companies

We'll refund all your money back or re-train your staff if they cannot:
- Train in less time than traditional training (basic, intermediate, advanced).
- Work like an expert straight from the classroom.
- Produce perfect results every time.

Accountancy Firm

FREE Three-Month Trial – No Risk Guarantee

For the first three months all Partner time will be absolutely FREE of charge. You don't pay us a single cent!

You also have access to our FREE telephone support helpline.

If you're not happy after three months with the additional services we provide such as payroll, bookkeeping, and tax returns, we will refund back to you all the fees you've paid.

Carpet Cleaning

If after cleaning your carpet you don't think it's the cleanest your carpet has looked since new, we'll clean it again. If you're still not satisfied, we'll refund your money in full!

Estate Agent

We promise to sell your house within 4 weeks. If we don't fulfil our promise, we'll give you R500. Yes, give YOU R500.

Why would we do this?

Because we sold 2344 houses last year. We believe in our ability to do our job. And our job is to sell your house. If we can't do our job, we firmly believe we should suffer not you. That's why we'll happily give you a cheque for R500 should we fail.

Printing Device Products

Here's my way of standing behind the Tri-Creaser 100%. The Tri-Creaser comes with this unique guarantee…

Unique Five-Tiered Risk-Free Guarantee

<u>**Guarantee 1:**</u> If your Tri-Creaser isn't as easy to use as we say it is — even the first time you use it, and doesn't save you hours of time, send it back for a full and courteous refund.

<u>**Guarantee 2:**</u> If your Tri-Creaser doesn't eliminate fiber cracking on materials ranging from 150-350 gsm — send it back for a full and courteous refund.

<u>**Guarantee 3:**</u> If after three whole months you are not satisfied with your Tri-Creaser for any reason, or no reason at all, send it back to us for a full and courteous refund.

<u>**Guarantee 4:**</u> If after 12 months your Tri- Creaser hasn't saved you more than 5 times the cost you paid, return it to us for a full and courteous refund. Just take a photo of the
Tri-Creaser on your folding machine before you send it back to demonstrate you at least tried it out.

<u>**Guarantee 5:**</u> The Tri-Creaser comes with a full 3-year workmanship guarantee. If for any reason the Tri-Creaser malfunctions in any way in the first three years, we'll replace it immediately — at no cost to you!

I think you'll agree no one in our industry is offering a guarantee as powerful as this. It's my vivid way of showing you the belief I have in the Tri-Creaser — and its ability to solve one of the major frustrations we've all faced over the years — FIBRE CRACKING!

Hopefully, these examples will have **stirred** up your thought processes.

Notice how comforting they are. If you were buying any of these products or services how would you feel about these companies? Would you be inclined to use their products or services?

That's the power of risk reversal. It makes the buying decision quite easy for the client or customer. It literally multiplies response when you start your lead generation system!

Remember anything is possible. You owe it to yourself to create a powerful risk reversal strategy. Your clients or customers will appreciate you on a much higher plane, and you'll **attract** many more of them as a result!

Now let's look at how to **construct** your own risk reversal strategy...

Constructing your own risk reversal strategy

Putting in place your own risk reversal strategy is quite **simple**. First you need to ask yourself the following questions and write the answers down...

1. Do I get many complaints about my product(s) or service(s) from my clients or customers?

If you don't get many complaints about your product or service, then risk reversal will **definitely** help you grow your business.

If you get lots of complaints, you'd better start putting things right. If you don't, you'll eventually go out of business or at least fail to generate the sales and profits you always dreamed of. <u>**Don't** use risk reversal until you have reduced your cost!</u>

2. What is the end result my clients or customers are getting from receiving my product(s) or service(s)?

Think about the main **result** your clients or customers get from receiving and using your product or service.

The result our clients get is **growth** and increased profits, which in turn increases the value of their business. Think about what it is your clients or customers really want from your product or service.

Once you've done that, ask yourself how can you guarantee they'll **receive** this result?

> **Please Note:**
> Don't forget your risk reversal should be completely focused on your chosen niche(s)!

3. **Do my competitors offer any guarantees? If they do, what are they?**
   Very **few** people have **grasped** the concept of risk reversal. But it is still worth finding out if any of your competitors offer guarantees or a risk reversal.
   You'll know the answer to this having conducted your competitor research! (You did do it didn't you?).
   If they do don't worry. Just work out how you can better it – and it's easy. For example, if they offer a 1-year money back guarantee, you offer a 3-year money back guarantee etc)!

4. **What are the three main things that can prevent my clients or customers from buying from me?**

   This really looks at the three main **objections** your clients or customers may have when appointing you. In many cases the three main objections when people are buying products or services are; Cost, doubts about expertise, and concern that you won't deliver the number one result they are seeking.

   If you can guarantee all these objections in some way – you're onto a real **winner**.

5. **What are the main three irritations/frustrations clients have about my industry in general? How can I overcome these?**

   Most industries have common irritations that people dislike. Accountants for example have a perceived poor reputation for charging clients for every single minute of their time – whether or not it's productive time.

   Think about what irritates your clients or customers and see if you can **overcome** these irritations.
   Delivering a risk reversal that ensures people's worries or irritations will not occur, is an immensely powerful approach.

6. **What is the pain or fear your clients or customers have?**

   Your product or service gives your clients or customers a result. But what "**pain**" could they have if your product or service wasn't **available**, or the product or service didn't **fulfil** its desired result.

   For example, the pain our clients would suffer if our business growth services weren't available is, they'd find it difficult to grow their businesses and increase profits to the levels they desire. They'd also find it almost impossible to increase the value of their businesses!

   Derivatives of this pain could be lack of money and less time to give the owner the freedom to choose what they want to do with their life etc.

   Go where the pain is and construct your risk reversal around it.

7. **What 'pain' or 'loss' can you inflict on yourself or your business if you don't follow through with your promises?**

   This is an especially important element of your risk reversal. Remember the simple 'formula' we showed you earlier…

What you want to do is penalize you or your business for not fulfilling the promises you set. This could be a monetary penalty, a service-oriented penalty (carry out service again at no cost), a product replacement penalty, or anything you can think of!

You should now have an excellent picture of what you can and can't include in your risk reversal. Now you just need to put it together and refine it until you have something people sit up and think – **wow**, I can't refuse this!

Just one word of advice…

When you put together your risk reversal try and **eliminate** any conditions. The more conditions you have – the less attractive your risk reversal will be.

For example, if we take the Estate Agent example…

> We promise to sell your house within 4 weeks. If we don't fulfil our promise, we'll give you R500. Yes, give YOU R500.
>
> Why would we do this?
>
> Because we sold 2344 houses last year. We believe in our ability to do our job. And our job is to sell your house. If we can't do our job, we firmly believe we should suffer not you. That's why we'll happily give you a cheque for R500 should we fail.

It would be extremely easy to put conditions to this risk reversal such as…
- As long as you accept any offer within 15% of the asking price
- As long as you keep the house clean and presentable
- As long as you make the changes, we've suggested
- The list could be endless!

When you add conditions, the result is worthless. Conditions show you're scared. They show you don't really value your product or service. That's why we've spent time to educate you on the real benefits of using risk reversal as an important business building principle and strategy. Understanding HOW risk reversal works will hopefully have allayed any of your fears.

Don't get frightened. Like we said earlier, if you are good at what you do, risk reversal will be an enormous success for you.

Now let's look at how you can **add** significant **power** to your risk reversal strategy by adding "Reasons Why" (another of our power packed 'Principles') …

You must give reasons why…

Every time you state your risk reversal you must **build** credibility and conviction. If you don't do this people will not believe what you're saying.

This is simple to achieve. All you do is give the reasons why you offer risk reversal in the first place.

Let's take these two examples – the estate agent and the accountant, and show you how to do it…

Estate Agents Reasons Why…

> Why would we do this?
>
> Because we sold 2344 houses last year. We believe in our ability to do our job. And our job is to sell your house. If we can't do our job, we firmly believe we should suffer not you. That's why we'll happily give you a cheque for R500 should we fail.

Accountant Reasons Why…

> 1. We don't want you to take any risk whatsoever when you start using our services.
>
> 2. We shoulder all the risk. If we don't live up to your high expectations, we suffer – not you.
>
> 3. We don't believe you should have to make the decision to appoint an accountancy firm after meeting the Partners on just one or two occasions. You will still have many unanswered questions in your mind. Therefore, we give you the opportunity and time to sample our services before committing yourself. This is as fair as we can be!

4. Accountancy services are "intangible." You only see the benefit of accountancy services once you start using them. Therefore, we give you three months to try our services and decide for yourself if we're right for you and your company. If we're not, simply tell us and we'll give you a courteous refund of all the fees you've paid.

5. A FREE three-month trial period is the best method we use to get new clients. Because we're very good at what we do, the three-month trial period helps us prove to you how good we are without any financial risk to you.

6. One common complaint with many accountancy firms is people don't think the Partners are proactive enough — giving suggestions to improve your business, tax saving advice etc. Our clients have told us they value our commitment to this. The FREE three-month trial period gives you enough time to judge for yourself how forward thinking we really are in this area.

Do you see how powerful this is? Not only have they created a strong risk reversal, they've cemented the sales argument by explaining why they offer risk reversal in the first place.

Hopefully, you can see how powerful the risk reversal becomes when you attach reasons why.

Notice there is no pre-determined length to the reasons why. You just need to credibly explain why you offer your risk reversal – so your prospects and clients or customers believe what you're saying, and it has credibility.

———————————

Start working on your risk reversal – now!

All it costs you is time. The effort you put in will be rewarded significantly.

We guarantee you'll start attracting more and more clients or customers to your business, as **soon** as you **implement** your own risk reversal strategy.

The XBS Programme
Module 8 Fonts

Making your advertising and marketing communications easy to read to ensure the highest response

Introduction

What we're about to say will surprise – even shock you...

The type of font and the size of the font you use in your advertising and marketing communications can have a huge **influence** on the success of your lead generation program.

Whether it's in sales letters, adverts, Special Reports, leaflets, web site or any other type of lead generation method, the font you use can result in your communication being easy, or conversely difficult to read.

> **Remember, in every case, you want the reader to read as much as possible in the quickest time.**
> **Achieve this and you automatically gain more high-quality leads!**

Numerous studies (notably by Dr Rudolf Flesch) have shown how the choice of font can increase or decrease a person's ability to read passages of text. In fact, some fonts can actually force a reader to give up!

Therefore, perhaps surprisingly, your choice of font can have a positive or negative influence on the number of leads you generate!

There are three main types of fonts available to you...
1. Serif fonts
2. Sans Serif fonts
3. Script fonts

Let's now explore each font and how you should **use** them...

Serif Fonts

(for all body copy, long headlines, and subheads)

You can spot a Serif font from the tiny little **'feet'** on the bottom of the letters. These feet actually help guide your eye across the page, making passages of text very easy to read.

From an early age we are **conditioned** to read this type of font. You'll notice all children's books are set using Serif fonts.

Consequently, you should use Serif fonts for the body copy of all your marketing communications (<u>except</u> your web site), and long headlines.

Examples of Serif fonts…
- Book Antiqua
- Bookman Old style
- Times New Roman
- Courier
- Century Schoolbook

Sans Serif Fonts

(for short headlines, subheads, and labels, and web site copy)

Sans Serif basically means 'without feet.' They are much harder to read than Serif fonts and should therefore only be used for headlines, subheads, short captions, and labels.

Don't ever set body copy in a Sans Serif font. It may look pleasing to the eye, but I guarantee your reader will find it much harder to read. In fact, tests have shown that using a Sans Serif font can reduce the ease of reading by as much as 40%.

Examples of Sans Serif fonts…

> **Please Note:**
> There is one exception. For some reason sans serif fonts are easier to read on a web site. Therefore, the body copy of your web site should be set in a sans serif font such as 'Verdana.'

- News Gothic
- Tahoma
- Arial
- Century Gothic
- Eras light
- Eurostyle
- Verdana

Script Fonts

(for invitations, addresses on envelopes etc)

Script fonts give the impression of personal handwriting. Generally speaking, they shouldn't be used in business to business writing except for invitations, or other special occasions.

You can however use a script font to good effect by imitating personal handwriting in the margins of sales letters, or in the P.S. of a letter.

Examples of Script fonts are…
- Monotype Corsiva
- Lucida Handwriting
- Bradley Hand ITC
- French Script

How to choose your "ideal" fonts

Now you know the importance of fonts, you should standardize all your documentation. That means your lead generation tools (such as ads and sales letters) need the perfect fonts!

> **Please Note:**
> Clearly, we are concentrating on lead generation here, but it is a worthwhile exercise to change your internal documentation such as letters to clients or customers etc to meet the conditions we give you below.

First you need to choose two fonts – a Serif font for your body copy and long headlines, and a Sans Serif font for your short headlines and subheads.

We've set a paragraph below in several of the best and easy to read Serif fonts, followed by some of the better Sans Serif fonts. (We've also shown examples of Script fonts for your information).

Simply go through each Serif and Sans Serif font and decide which ones you prefer. Then choose one of your own letters and apply the selected fonts to it. Print each letter off and decide which fonts you like best.

At this stage you may want other people in your business to offer their **opinion** on a couple of your favorites.

Serif Fonts (set in 12 point) …

Baskerville Old Face

My message here is that what marketers have forgotten and need to remember real soon is that marketing is about selling stuff. Marketing is not about creating an image. Having an image just means that I know who you are, but it doesn't motivate me to do anything. Marketing is not about creating award-winning commercials either. It is about having programs and promotions and advertising and a million other things that are effective at convincing people that they should buy your products or services. It is about profit. It is about results! - Sergio Zyman author of "The End Of Marketing As We Know It".

Bell MT

My message here is that what marketers have forgotten and need to remember real soon is that marketing is about selling stuff.
Marketing is not about creating an image. Having an image just means that I know who you are, but it doesn't motivate me to do anything. Marketing is not about creating award-winning commercials either. It is about having programs and promotions and advertising and a million other things that are effective at convincing people that they should buy your products or services. It is about profit. It is about results! - Sergio Zyman author of "The End Of Marketing As We Know It"

Book Antiqua

My message here is that what marketers have forgotten and need to remember real soon is that marketing is about selling stuff. Marketing is not about creating an image. Having an image just means that I know who you are, but it doesn't motivate me to do anything. Marketing is not about creating award-winning commercials either. It is about having programs and promotions and advertising and a million other things that are effective at convincing people that they should buy your products or services. It is about profit. It is about results! - Sergio Zyman author of "The End Of Marketing As We Know It"

Bookman Oldstyle

My message here is that what marketers have forgotten and need to remember real soon is that marketing is about selling stuff. Marketing is not about creating an image. Having an image just means that I know who you are, but it doesn't motivate me to do anything. Marketing is not about creating award-winning commercials either. It is about having programs and promotions and advertising and a million other things that are effective at convincing people that they should buy your products or services. It is about profit. It is about results! - Sergio Zyman author of "The End Of Marketing As We Know It"

Calisto MT

My message here is that what marketers have forgotten and need to remember real soon is that marketing is about selling stuff.
Marketing is not about creating an image. Having an image just means that I know who you are, but it doesn't motivate me to do anything. Marketing is not about creating award-winning commercials either. It is about having programs and promotions and advertising and a million other things that are effective at convincing people that they should buy your products or services. It is about profit. It is about results! - Sergio Zyman author of "The End Of Marketing As We Know It"

Century Schoolbook

My message here is that what marketers have forgotten and need to remember real soon is that marketing is about selling stuff. Marketing is not about creating an image. Having an image just means that I know who you are, but it doesn't motivate me to do anything. Marketing is not about creating award-winning commercials either. It is about having programs and promotions and advertising and a million other things that are effective at convincing people that they should buy your products or services. It is about profit. It is about results! - Sergio Zyman author of "The End Of Marketing As We Know It"

Courier New

My message here is that what marketers have forgotten and need to remember real soon is that marketing is about selling stuff.
Marketing is not about creating an image. Having an image just means that I know who you are, but it doesn't motivate me to do anything. Marketing is not about creating award-winning commercials either. It is about having programs and promotions and advertising and a million other things that are effective at convincing people that they should buy your products or services. It is about profit. It is about results! - Sergio Zyman author of "The End Of Marketing As We Know It"

Garamond

My message here is that what marketers have forgotten and need to remember real soon is that marketing is about selling stuff. Marketing is not about creating an image. Having an image just means that I know who you are, but it doesn't motivate me to do anything. Marketing is not about creating award-winning commercials either. It is about having programs and promotions and advertising and a million other things that are effective at convincing people that they should buy your products or services. It is about profit. It is about results! - Sergio Zyman author of "The End Of Marketing As We Know It"

Goudy Old Style

My message here is that what marketers have forgotten and need to remember real soon is that marketing is about selling stuff. Marketing is not about creating an image. Having an image just means that I know who you are, but it doesn't motivate me to do anything. Marketing is not about creating award-winning commercials either. It is about having programs and promotions and advertising and a million other things that are effective at convincing people that they should buy your products or services. It is about profit. It is about results! - Sergio Zyman author of "The End Of Marketing As We Know It"

Guatemala

My message here is that what marketers have forgotten and need to remember real soon is that marketing is about selling stuff.
Marketing is not about creating an image. Having an image just means that I know who you are, but it doesn't motivate me to do anything. Marketing is not about creating award-winning commercials either. It is about having programs and promotions and advertising and a million other things that are effective at convincing people that they should buy your products or services. It is about profit. It is about results! - Sergio Zyman author of "The End Of Marketing As We Know It"

Times New Roman

My message here is that what marketers have forgotten and need to remember real soon is that marketing is about selling stuff. Marketing is not about creating an image. Having an image just means that I know who you are, but it doesn't motivate me to do anything.
Marketing is not about creating award-winning commercials either. It is about having programs and promotions and advertising and a million other things that are effective at convincing people that they should buy your products or services. It is about profit. It is about results! - Sergio Zyman author of "The End Of Marketing As We Know It"

Sans Serif Fonts (set in 12 point) ...

Arial

Who Else Wants A Screen Star Figure?

Century Gothic

Who Else Wants A Screen Star Figure?

Eurostyle

Who Else Wants A Screen Star Figure?

Franklin Gothic Book

Who Else Wants A Screen Star Figure?

Lucida Console

Who Else Wants A Screen Star Figure?

Lucida Sans

Who Else Wants A Screen Star Figure?

News Gothic MT

Who Else Wants A Screen Star Figure?

Tahoma

Who Else Wants A Screen Star Figure?

Verdana

Who Else Wants A Screen Star Figure?

Script Fonts (set in 12 point) ...

Bradley Hand ITC

Your Personal Invitation Enclosed...

Brush Script MT

Your Personal Invitation Enclosed...

French Script MT

Your Personal Invitation Enclosed...

Lucida Handwriting

Your Personal Invitation Enclosed…

Monotype Corsiva

Your Personal Invitation Enclosed…

Viner Hand ITC

Your Personal Invitation Enclosed…

What Size Font Should You Use?

Now you've chosen the fonts you like; you now need to set a size to them. This is especially important for your body copy font (Serif font – except on your web site).

As a basic guideline anything less than 10 point makes it too hard to read. Choose a font size of 11, 12, or 13, to be on the safe side. If your clients tend to be more elderly, you may want to choose a font size of 13 to 15. This whole program is set in 12 point.

> **Please Note:**
> Where this 'general rule' does get broken is in print advertising (newspapers, magazines, trade magazines, Yellow Pages etc). Because you have severe limitations on space you may have to drop your font size down to 8 or 9. We generally use Times New Roman in our ads because Times is a narrow font so allows more copy to be included.

Also, you'll have noticed that some fonts are smaller than others due to the formation of the letters. Simply adjust the size accordingly.

Now you've selected your Serif font, your Sans Serif font, and font size, you must ensure you and ALL the people in your business use these fonts and ONLY these fonts. You must create the same "look and feel" and consistency throughout your company!

Module 9 Testimonials

Helping you generate many more leads, by proving you can deliver on your promises!

Introduction

Because your prospects only see the true benefit of your product or service, days, weeks, months, or even years down the line, they need to believe you can do exactly what you say you can!

If they don't believe you – then you don't get the lead. If you don't get the lead you don't get the sale. It's as simple as that!

Testimonials are unbelievably valuable for this reason – they convince the prospect you can deliver on your promises. They also help to build credibility and add value to your product or service.

Here's what a couple of highly respected marketing legends have said about testimonials…

> "The reader finds it easier to believe the endorsement of a fellow consumer than the puffery of an anonymous copywriter" - **David Ogilvy**, Confessions of an Advertising Man, 1963

> "Every type of advertiser has the same problem: to be believed. The mail order man knows nothing so potent for this purpose as the testimonial, yet the general advertiser seldom uses it" – **James Webb Young** (one of the best copywriters in history).

So, what exactly is a testimonial?

A testimonial is simply a statement of praise from a satisfied client or customer (or sometimes a celebrity).

Let's now look at what makes a powerful testimonial…

What makes a testimonial powerful and effective?

Using any testimonial is better than using none. However, you can make your testimonials much more effective.

More effective means more leads. More leads means more sales, more new clients or customers, and more profit!

Follow these proven guidelines…

1. Identify persons giving testimonials by their name, their title, what they do, and where they're from

If you can't put the details of the person providing the testimonial, you're better off not using it – they arouse suspicion!

2. Make sure your testimonials are specific

For example, consider how weak these testimonials are. This is how most companies use testimonials…

- "The power of this is truly amazing" (what was the power and what did it consist of?)
- "I'm delighted to say that this workshop has made a significant difference" (A difference in what?)
- "Very interesting and informative" (what did you learn and what was interesting about it?)

Instead of saying "It doesn't cost much" say "It costs less than the price of a pint of beer"

Words like 'wonderful' and 'brilliant' are nowhere near as effective as a precise description of what the service has done for the person.

Give exact figures and percentages. Don't just say, "Our business made more profit." Say, "Our business made R24,900 more profit after using ABC Services."

3. Is the testimonial positive?

Make sure the testimonial is positive. "Not a waste of money" for example, could do more harm than good. Change it around – "Every cent spent was worth it" would be much more positive.

4. Is the testimonial clear?

Make sure the testimonial reads well and is clear to the reader.

5. The Amazing Secret Nobody Uses – Put the telephone number, e-mail address or web address at the end of the testimonial

This technique really does make a big difference. If you can put the telephone number or the e-mail address or the web address (in that order of importance) of the person providing the testimonial. This adds incredible strength and believability to your testimonial.

Surprisingly, the clients providing their contact details won't be contacted frequently. The fact that the contact information is provided, is usually enough to convince your prospects that the testimonial is real and believable.

Better still…

Those clients that are called will do your selling for you!

We've rarely seen this technique used, yet it is the key to successful and very powerful testimonials.

Please note if you are selling to the consumer it may be better to provide their e-mail address, rather than their telephone number.

6. Get testimonials from both sexes

Don't alienate one of the sexes. Make sure you get testimonials from both sexes (unless of course your product or service only applies to one of the sexes!).

7. A testimonial should always be enclosed by quotation marks

"This shows to your prospect that your client has actually said these things."

8. A testimonial is stronger when it is accompanied by the photo of the testimonial giver

This of course is more difficult in practice, but well worth the effort.

9. Testimonials don't have to come solely from clients or customers

Sometimes even more important testimonials can come from publishers, and any other form of media. If people say good things about you, they can provide powerful testimonials whether they're clients or not!

10. Each testimonial should vary from the next to enable you to match testimonials to the prospect's circumstances

This is especially important. What you need to do is get three or four paragraphs (if possible). Each paragraph vividly describes one major benefit (and of course the USP) of your product or service.

You can then use one testimonial for four different circumstances.

Don't worry if you can't get each testimonial to cover more than one benefit. Just make sure the testimonials you use focuses on one different benefit so together they prove everything you're saying!

11. Try to get your testimonials on different formats

Most of the time we give testimonials out on paper form. That's great but just think of the added impact you can create if you put the testimonial on audio or even better on video!

If your client will allow you to video a live testimonial you can use this to fantastic effect especially in your sales presentations and in your reception area. Use technology to your advantage it really will make a difference!

Get your client to specify how long you worked together, the products or services you provided, the specific results you achieved, their importance to the client or customer, and the general industry conditions at the time.

How to get testimonials

Okay, you know what makes a good testimonial. Now you have to get them. Here are the proven methods for collecting testimonials for your business.

Don't worry.

Contrary to popular belief, it's very simple to get testimonials…

- Ask for a testimonial straight after completing some work for the client

If the client is clearly happy with you say, "You know, I'm really happy that we were able to work with you. It would be really helpful if you could send me a letter, on your letterhead with a few comments about our product or service. Would that be okay?"

Your satisfied client or customer will usually be honored with such a request. If you don't receive the testimonial in the next 10 days (this is quite common because they haven't had time, and it's not high priority for them) ring them up and offer to write the letter for them using the technique described next.

- Writing the testimonial, yourself with a helping hand from your client or customer

This is an excellent way to get powerful testimonials. Here's how to do it…

Call your client or customer up and say something like, "We're putting together a number of testimonials from our best clients. Would you mind providing one for us?"

Then say, "I can write the testimonial for you. All you have to do is check it and agree it. What I'd prefer though is if you could quickly write down two or three specific benefits you've received from using our product or service, and either e-mail or post them to me. I'll then write the testimonial including these points."

By doing this you will usually get some specific facts in the clients or customers words to add power to your testimonial

- Unsolicited testimonial letters

  You will get letters of praise without having to ask for them as long as you make a positive difference to people.

  However, you can increase the probability of receiving these types of testimonials.

  For example, you can say to all your clients or customers when they place an order "Please let us know how our product or service has benefited you in a couple of weeks."

- Contests

  A great way to get testimonials is to run a contest offering a prize (cash or other) for the best letters telling, "Why I like (name of your product/service)." Or "Finish this sentence in twenty-five words or less: I like (name of product/service) because…"

- Feedback Sheets and Questionnaires

  Provide clients with postage paid postcards to mail back to you with their comments.

  Ask attendees at your seminar to fill out an evaluation form before they go home. To get the best testimonials, don't use rating scale questions such as "poor-fair- good-very good" – use open ended specific questions such as:

  1. How would you characterize the product/service at…?

  2. What changes have happened in your life or business as a result of receiving (name of your product/service) …?

  3. What were the three most valuable things you learnt today…?

  4. How did you like your…?

  5. What results would you attribute to having used our…?

  6. Based on your experience would you recommend our … product/service to other companies?

  7. What would you tell other … who are considering using our … product/service?

  8. What do you like about the way we do things?

  9. What do you dislike about the way we do things?

  10.   Is there anything else you can tell me to help me improve things for you?

  If you do use (or have used) questionnaires with rating scales, you can then modify the data to suit you.

  For example, if everyone states that they would recommend you to their friends, colleagues etc say "100% of our clients said they would recommend us to their colleagues."

- Well Known People Famous clients or customers will help greatly. It doesn't have to be well known personalities. It can include well-known companies. Simply by listing well-known companies who use your product or service adds conviction, credibility, and believability.

If you can get a famous person to recommend your product or service this adds great impact also.

However, be careful. Sometimes the personality becomes remembered and the product or service forgotten. Also don't forget you will usually have to pay an endorsement fee for this.

For example, 'POLICE Sunglasses' paid soccer star David Beckham a reported R1m to endorse their sunglasses. The result was a twelve-fold increase in sales – money very well spent!

- Conversational comments

    If someone offers you spontaneous praise in a meeting or on the phone ask, "Can I quote you on that?" Immediately write down what was said and get permission to use it.

- Using facts that do a good job in addition to testimonials

    You can also use specific facts that carry the power of testimonials. For example, …

    1. Ninety five percent of clients come back and order from us

    2. Every client we have served has increased profits by a minimum of R15,000

- If you sell your product or service to consumers from a restaurant or retail outlet for example, give your clients or customers a "Testimonial Card"

    Ask them to write something nice about your product or service and include a tick box to give you permission to use it. (Thank them with a discount or small gift.)

    When you make a sale, ask the client to write on the back of their business card or testimonial card (if you sell to consumers) the reason why they bought from you

    This will provide a unique way of having mini testimonials that you can file and show to prospects.

- A clever way of using testimonials is to have a client speak at one of your seminars for 4 or 5 minutes on how they use your product or service and the results they've had. They can then be open to questions from the attendees Incidentally, this is one of the most powerful things you can do at a seminar!

- If you've received a letter or had a verbal thanks from a client and you didn't ask them there and then if you could use their comments you can write with the following letter (or something similar):

> Dear John,
>
> I never did get round to thanking you for your letter of *date* (copy attached). So, thanks!
>
> I'd like to quote from this letter in the brochures, direct mail packages, advertising, PR and other marketing materials I use to promote my ABC Product/Service - with your permission of course. If this is okay with you, would you please sign the bottom of this letter and send it back to me in the enclosed envelope.
>
> Many thanks.
>
> Kind regards
>
>
> Your Name
>
> You have my permission to quote from the attached letter in ads, brochures, direct mail, pr and other marketing materials to promote your service.
>
> Signature
>
> Date

Always send a stamped addressed envelope and two copies of the letter.

If you'd rather not ask for testimonials the following 'Testimonial Gathering Letter' is an excellent and very quick way to solicit favourable testimonials (this is awesome!):

> Good Morning John,
> I have a favor to ask of you.

> I'm in the process of putting together a list of testimonials — a collection of comments about my ABC Product/Service, from satisfied clients like yourself.
>
> Would you take a few minutes to give me your opinion of my ABC Product/Service? No need to dictate a letter —just jot your comments on the back of this letter, and I'll put it into context. I'll then send it back to you for approval.
>
> I look forward to learning what you like about my ABC Product/Service... but I also welcome any suggestions or criticisms too. Many thanks.
>
> Kind regards
>
> Your Name
>
> You have my permission to quote from the attached letter in ads, brochures, direct mail, pr and other marketing materials to promote your service.
>
> Signature
>
> Date

(**Please note:** This letter urges good and bad feedback, which shows you want the information to serve your clients or customers better in the future)

Changing testimonials

Don't worry about changing testimonials written by clients or customers. Make them snappier and more specific, and then ask them for their permission to use them.

Ask your client or customer for approval of the revised version. Do it diplomatically:

> "Dave, I'm really grateful for what you wrote about our product/service. Would it be okay if we cut the sentence about... and added the fact...?"

Using testimonials

Now you've got your testimonials you need to start using them to help you **gain** more leads, more sales and more clients or customers. As a rule, you can't use testimonials enough. And you can't ever have enough of them.

Knowing that testimonials are an important part of getting new clients or customers, you should use them in **every** interaction you have with your prospects and clients or customers. So, let's look at some of the applications…

1. Use testimonials in <u>ALL</u> your lead generation tools

2. Use testimonials in your sales presentation

3. Use testimonials written to counter objections

   This is an enormously powerful concept. Write testimonials in a way that they overcome your common objections.

   When a prospect brings up the objection, simply say, "I understand. Actually, John Brown of ABC Associates raised the same point. He's now a customer. Do you mind if I show you what he's written?"

   You then get the testimonial out – and hey presto – no more difficult objections to handle!

4. In your company brochure

5. On the wall of your reception area and/or in a 'Testimonial Book' placed on a table in your reception area (or both). Make sure you don't leave any other reading material in your reception area. This ethically 'forces' people to read your testimonial book!

   It is much better to have your' Testimonial Book' in your reception area than newspapers or other publications.

   We guarantee people will find opening it irresistible

6. You can use testimonials very effectively to knock the competition (ethically) without changing the facts. For example, to **highlight** your uniqueness…

   Instead of saying:

   "ABC Company have a free Client Advice Line." Say:

> "**Unlike other accountants ABC Company provide a Client Advice Line. It's free to use and you don't pay a single cent discussing any financial matter with a partner no matter how long the call lasts.**"

This quickly highlights your uniqueness and your USP by suggesting **no other** accountants offer a Client Advice Line.

Basically, you **can't** go wrong if you remember this…

> "Use testimonials in every marketing communication you have with your prospects and you'll get more leads, more sales and more clients or customers - guaranteed!"

Module 10 Irresistible Offers

How to multiply your sales and profits using irresistible offers

Introduction

Have we got a treat for you right now? What you're going to discover is how to create an irresistible offer that multiplies the success of your lead generation program, and ultimately helps you get more clients or customers than you ever thought possible.

This is an especially important Module for you. This one strategy alone can take your business to levels you never thought were possible. So, make sure you get at least an hour of uninterrupted time. Make no mistake if you get this right you'll never look back ever again!

First, we need to explain a few fundamentals – 'Cost of Client Acquisition' and 'Lifetime Customer Value (LCV)' (one of the XBS Business Growth Principles
– remember?) …

Cost of Client Acquisition – And why it's so important to the success of your lead generation system

In a nutshell, 'cost of client acquisition' is the amount of money you are prepared to spend on lead generation to get a new client or customer.

What's significant when selling most products or services is that your cost of client acquisition can be relatively **high**.

This is a **good** thing. It means you can afford to spend more to acquire leads in the first place. The result is a sharp increase in leads and consequently new clients or customers.

First, you need to work out the 'lifetime customer value' of your clients or customers.

Quite simply lifetime value is the average profit a client or customer generates whilst they maintain a relationship with you. (Using the Quantum Keys will massively increase and multiply this value, by the way!).

A good guide to use is 5 years for the duration (but you'll know what your average lifetime is).

Let's say one new client or customer generates R1,000 per year for 5 years. And your gross margin is 50%. That means your average lifetime value over 5 years is R2,500 (and this figure here doesn't include referrals (another Quantum Key) which you should also factor in).

Now let's say you currently use sales letters as one of your lead generation tools to generate new clients or customers (amongst loads of other lead generation marketing tools we'll discuss shortly!). And you generate one client or customer from 100 letters that cost in total R200.

This means your cost of client acquisition is R200. If you get 2 clients from the above scenario your cost of client acquisition would be R100, and so on.

This means you're left with R2,300 (your gross profit minus your cost of client acquisition). That's pretty **good**.

Here's how you can use this to your favor. Listen up, because this will have a huge impact on your business...

First if you know that for every R200 you spend to generate a new client or customer, it results in new profit of R2,300 - you should do **more** of it - much more!

Second in this example above you should test your sales letter ('Testing' is discussed shortly) because if you increased response to two or three percent your success would double or triple for the same time, effort, and cost.

And finally, the key to your success is to increase your cost of client acquisition so it makes it impossible for prospects to say 'no.'

Just think what would happen if you spent say R400 or even R600 on your sales piece/offer? Your leads and new client acquisitions would **multiply** literally overnight.

This could include 'buying' your clients by giving important products or services to them for free or for a vastly reduced rate; including bonus gifts once they become a client.

Or this could mean spending more money on your sales piece by using an eye-catching free gift with the mailing or some kind of gimmick.

All these things will help to multiply response and generate many more clients. This is an enormously powerful concept – we call it creating IRRESISTIBLE OFFERS!

> **Please Note:**
> What's great about this strategy is that your competitors won't understand what you're doing.
>
> They'll think you must be mad.

> What they won't understand is that you've leveraged your business many times because you're concentrating on the profit you'll generate over the course of the relationship and NOT on the profit you make on the first sale!

Do you see the power of this? Do you now see the significant shift in thinking you've just taken?

You've gone from – How much money did we make on the **first** order?

To…

How much money have we made over the **duration** of the relationship?

This is a massive difference!

To make things clearer here's an illustration showing the **difference** in the two approaches…

Let's say you send a sales letter out to 500 people in your niche market.

Here's a breakdown of the costs (to keep things simple we haven't included any costs relating to meeting the prospect or preparing and sending quotes etc) …

Expense Item	Cost
Postage	R135
Printing of 3-page letter	R50
Business reply cards	R50
Letterheads	R40
Continuation Sheets	R50
Envelopes	R10
TOTAL	**R335**

> **Please Note:**
> We haven't mentioned this at all so far, but you'll have noticed all the way through these first 141 pages or so, we talk about 'high quality' leads.

> As you know there's a significant difference between generating 'any kind' of leads and 'good quality' leads.
>
> So how do we know you'll generate high quality leads? Simple. You've done all the preparation work (so far). In particular you've chosen your niche market(s), which means all your leads (or a very high proportion of them) will be high quality valuable leads!

1. Using the **'traditional'** method for evaluating the success of your lead generation tool

From this letter you generate 10 high quality leads (2%).

And of these 10 you get 2 new clients or customers (you haven't yet focused on Sales Conversion!) worth R400 each on the first order.

That's a total income of R800. If your gross margin is 50% that means you've generated R400 from a cost of R335 – i.e. you've made R65. That's close to the bone, but at least you've made a profit.

Here's how it looks…

Lead Generation Tool: Sales Letter	Amount
Leads Generated	10
Clients Gained	2
First Sale Value Per Client	R400.00
Total Income Generated	R800.00
Gross Margin	50%
Gross Profit	R400.00
Total Cost	R335.00
Net Profit	**R65.00**

With this example most people would conclude the lead generation tool isn't profitable enough to run again. We could increase the 'cost of client acquisition' to give us a better chance but that would mean we'd be going into a loss-making situation.

So, what happens? Yes, you stop using this lead generation tool. **BIG BIG** MISTAKE.

Here's why...

    2. Using 'cost of client acquisition' to evaluate the success of your lead generation tool

Your average 'lifetime value' is R1000 per client. Now let's see how it all looks...

Lead Generation Tool: Sales Letter	Amount
Leads Generated	10
Clients Gained	2
Average Lifetime Value	R1,000
Total Income Generated	R2,000
Gross Margin	(already taken into account with Lifetime Value)
Total Cost	R335.00
Net Profit	**R1,665.00**

Now we have a completely **different** picture. A lead generation tool that seemed to be 'poor' is actually giving you a return on investment (ROI) of almost 5 times. That's pretty good by anyone's standards.

Now we can increase the cost of client acquisition because the **margin** is there. By increasing the cost of client acquisition we're allowing ourselves to create an **IRRESISTIBLE OFFER.**

And don't forget when you increase your cost of client acquisition what you're doing is increasing your response. More leads means more clients and so on.

You can now keep running that same sales letter **until** it stops giving you a return on your investment – this may never actually happen. Ads and letters can keep on working for years and years!

So how do you create an Irresistible Offer?

As we said earlier, an irresistible offer is 'born' out of combining the dual power of 'cost of client acquisition' and 'lifetime customer value.'

What you've discovered so far during this Module is that in reality you have the ability to 'bribe' prospects into becoming clients or customers, because you're not focusing on the first sale, but on the amount of profit over the duration of the relationship with your customer.

In short - you have much more money to spend than you ever thought to acquire new customers.

Clearly it takes you time to generate the lifetime profit (i.e. over the lifetime of the relationship) so you **still need to keep an eye on your cash flow.**

But be sensible and what you have is an unstoppable lead generation program that your competitors can't hope to compete with (because they don't understand what you're doing!).

3 Great Irresistible Offers That Always Work For Any Business Are...

- FREE Trials Of Your Product Or Service (the best offer)
- FREE Special Reports (another favorite of ours)
- FREE Additional Products/Services

Now to you these offers won't seem 'irresistible.' That's because you're too attached to your business. However, your potential clients or customers really do find these offers irresistible.

As long as you've followed the XBS Program so far, and chosen the perfect niche market(s), for example, we guarantee your prospects, and your clients or customers are going to be attracted to your offer.

Using Cost of Client Acquisition and Lifetime Customer Value, you can now tailor your irresistible offer to the 'budget' you've allowed. It really is quite simple.

The key is to think...

'What can I offer my prospects that they simply can't refuse'?

Or in the words of film – The Godfather, 'I'm going to make him an offer he can't refuse'

> **Caution**
>
> Don't get trapped into discounting your products or services. This is NOT what we're talking about. Discounts never have a lasting effect and only cheapen your products and services and worse still result in big decreases in profits.
>
> When you use the powerful strategies contained in the XBS Program, you should maintain (even increase) your prices/fees. The key is to create an offer that allows your prospects to 'sample' your products or services and expertise, so they are highly motivated to continue using them at the full price!

With this in mind, here's a proven 6 figure profit letter that focuses on an irresistible offer. We'll show you the letter in full and then give you the 'Fill-In-The-Blank Template' that you can use and apply.

As you'll soon discover the irresistible offer is a 'free lunch' which is a perfect 'sample' of the catering service this company provide.

Notice there's no mention of prices or discounts. And yes, to the owner of the business – this didn't seem to be an irresistible offer to her – but as you'll see – it was very desirable to her potential customers.

The premise behind this irresistible offer and the ones you'll create is this...

If you're good at what you do, people will flock to you once they've sampled your expertise and products or services. That's why free samples and Special Reports are so effective!

Here's the exact letter used, followed by the 'Fill-In-The- Blank Template'...

"Are You Planning A Business Meeting That Requires Fresh High-Quality Food At A Very Reasonable Price?"

"Order Your FREE O'Brien's Five Star Sandwich Platter"

Dear <Name> Here's

the deal:

You can receive a delicious O'Brien's Five Star Sandwich Platter (serves five people) - totally FREE. Or you can deduct the cost from your first order.

I'm not talking about your standard "buffet" food. I'm talking about high quality food made daily from fresh produce. I'm talking about presentation and packaging that makes in instant impact on people. Perfect for any meeting or special occasion with staff, associates, or clients/customers.

So why am I doing this?

Quite simply I've found that as soon as people taste our food and see our presentation and packaging, they're hooked. Nothing compares to this. They love it! And I've learnt that by providing a free platter we stand a better chance of getting your business in the long run.

I suppose the "proof of the pudding is in the eating". You can instantly form your own impression, having sampled our food. And that's it. No strings. No obligation.

Frankly, our platters are not for everyone. If you're not concerned about the impact your food has on your staff, associates and clients/customers, then we aren't for you. If, on the other hand you deeply appreciate the importance of having superbly presented high quality food and the positive impact this creates, then I urge you to call our FREEPHONE Platter Hotline on <Phone Number>.

So, what's the catch?

Well there isn't one - as long as you respond quickly.

Clearly, I can't keep this offer open indefinitely. You must reply before Friday 6th July to get your FREE Five Star Platter. So, the quicker you reply the less likely you are to be disappointed!

> **Why should you even try us out?**
>
> I appreciate the offer of a "free lunch" may not be enough to persuade you to place your order. After all, I know how important your meetings can be. However, I consider us the only specialist caterers for the business market in Leicester. Sure, other companies do it - but have they really thought about your real needs and wants. For example, do they offer? ...
>
> - A guarantee to deliver on time...
>
> **Guarantee 1:** We will deliver your entire order on time or you don't pay us a single cent
>
> **Guarantee 2:** If we do deliver your order late, your next meal is FREE (to the same value as your original order)
>
> - A varied and delicious menu with 10 choices of bread, choice of drinks (hot or cold), and catering for vegetarians
>
> - An instant meal where the food arrives ready for presentation on your tables
>
> - Catering for 5 to 5,000 people
>
> We offer all this as "standard." How many people do you think would be willing to offer such a guarantee? But that's the point. We guarantee on time delivery because we know how important this is to you. If we fail, we suffer
> - not you. Isn't that how it should be?
>
> I'm sure you can now appreciate why I think you should take advantage of my FREE offer. Do it now. Call our FREEPHONE Platter Hotline on
> **<Phone Number>**. We are eagerly awaiting your call.
>
> Kind regards
>
>
> Rosemary McIvor, Managing Director
>
> P.S Don't delay. This offer is only available until July 6th. Call me now on our FREEPHONE Platter Hotline on <Phone Number>. Thank you.
>
> P.P.S FREE DELIVERY! Whether your meeting is early in the morning, at lunchtime, or in the evening we will deliver to you FREE of charge!

This two-page letter is responsible for 6 figure profits in less than a year!

Now it's your turn to benefit. Here's the 'Fill-In-The-Blank Template' you can use.

All you do is fill-in-the-blanks (you'll find it easier if you compare what's written in the actual letter above at each section) ...

"Are You <enter the main benefit of your product or service, or the main problem it solves>?"

"<State the offer>"

Dear <Name>

Here's the deal:

You can receive <state the offer>.

I'm not talking about standard <state your type of product or service>. I'm talking about <state your three biggest benefits>.

So why am I doing this?

Quite simply I've found that as soon as people sample our services and see our <3 main benefits written slightly differently than above>. Nothing compares to this. They love it! And I've learnt that by providing a free <state your offer> we stand a better chance of getting your business in the long run.

I suppose the "proof of the pudding is in the eating". You can instantly form your own impression, having sampled our <product/service>. And that's it. No strings. No obligation.

Frankly, our <name of offer> are/is not for everyone.

If you're not concerned about <the type of quality your product/service provides> then we aren't for you. If, on the other hand you deeply appreciate the importance of <main benefits go here>, then I urge you to call our FREEPHONE
<Name of offer> Hotline on <Phone number>.

So, what's the catch?

Well there isn't one - as long as you respond quickly. Clearly, I can't keep this offer open indefinitely. You must reply before <Date> to get your FREE <Name of offer>. So, the quicker you reply the less likely you are to be disappointed!

Why should you even try us out?

I appreciate the offer of a <Name of Offer> may not be enough to persuade you to <place your order/start using our products/services etc>.

> product/service>. However, I consider us the
> only specialist <what do you specialize in i.e.
> caterers for the business market in Leicester>.
> Sure, other companies do it - but have they
> really thought about your real needs and wants.
> For example do they offer? …
>
> - <State your guarantee>
>
> - <List of benefits>
>
> We offer all this as "standard." How many
> people do you think would be willing to offer
> such a guarantee? But that's the point. We
> guarantee <state what you guarantee> because we
> know how important this is to you. If we fail,
> we suffer - not you. Isn't that how it should
> be?
>
> I'm sure you can now appreciate why I think you
> should take advantage of my FREE offer. Do it
> now. Call our FREEPHONE <Name of offer> Hotline
> on <Phone number>. We are eagerly awaiting your
> call.
>
> Kind regards
>
> <Your name> <Your title>
>
> P.S. Don't delay. This offer is only available
> until <Date>. Call me now on our FREEPHONE
> <Name of offer> Hotline on <Phone number>.
> Thank you.

Can you see how differently this will make you approach your lead generation in the future (starting tomorrow)?

Be sensible and what you have is an unstoppable lead generation program, that your competitors can't hope to compete with (because they don't understand what you're doing!).

Module 11

Lead Generation Strategy

How to maximise your response (and minimize your costs) by carefully matching your lead generation tools to your target or niche market(s)

Introduction

From today you're going to start thinking very clearly about the lead generation tools you SHOULD be using. That's likely to be a very different outcome to the tools you're using at the MOMENT.

We're going to explain the following critical things...
1. HOW to choose the lead generation tools that are most likely to give you the best return for every Rand you spend
2. How to decide if you should use irresistible offers up-front or later in the sales process (we discussed creating irresistible offers in the last XBS Module)
3. And finally, we're going to reveal a brilliant strategy that will make everything you do at least 10 times more effective. And we've never heard any other 'marketing gurus' talk about this one thing – even though they also use it!

Ready? Let's go...

HOW to choose the lead generation tools that are most likely to give you the best return for EVERY Rand you spend

Listen up because this is especially important.

What we've found over the years is that very few people give any great thought to the types of lead generation tools they should be using. They adopt the same marketing tools as all their competitors are using.

This means two things...
- In most cases you're not using the best lead generation tools to attract **YOUR** target market or niche
- You're lead generation campaigns are wasteful – even if they are still profitable.

So how do you choose the right lead generation tools for your business?

The good news is that this is EASY, and you should have already done the 'work.'

Earlier when we discussed – 'Defining Your Niche or Target Market,' there were two important questions we asked. We've repeated them again for you here...

Can your message be given to them easily?

This is massive. If your chosen niche can't be reached easily and cost-effectively then drop them off your list.

Here's where they can be found easily...

- At home
- At work (what is their position in the company?)
- Meeting in their clubs and associations
- In the community
- Speak to a "list broker" to find out if these groups can be located on one or more mailing lists (99% of the time there will be a mailing list(s) available – no matter how obscure your niche may be!)

This is a particularly important part of your research. The good thing is that as long as you use a list broker – they'll do the work for you.

A list broker is just like an insurance broker. They are independent and have access to all the database lists on the market. Simply tell them what characteristics your niche market has, and they'll go away and tell you which lists would be appropriate to use. You only pay when you decide to order the list!

Please take this advice on board. List brokers are a welcome addition to your "team" of suppliers. Even if you think your niche is diverse, don't think a list can't be found. You'll be pleasantly surprised at the amount of lists available!

To find any good list broker, simply look in your Yellow Pages under the category of 'Direct Mail.' Or do a search on the Internet using the keyword phrase, 'list broker.'

What publications do they read?

Often, your niche will read certain newspapers, magazines, trade journals etc. If so, they are easily reached through advertising. Don't worry.

> **Using our proven advertising techniques will ensure your advertising becomes very profitable!).**

There is also one other question at this stage you need to ask yourself and it's this…

"How do your niche typically source your type of product/service?"

For example, if you're a plumber your niche is likely to source a plumber using the Yellow Pages. Do you see how your lead generation tools can start selecting themselves using this simple approach?

Plus, having identified where your niche or target market can be found, coupled with the types of publications they read, gives you ALL the information you need to choose the 'perfect' lead generation tools for your business.

For example, ...

> **How do my niche source my type of product or service?**
> - Yellow Pages – you must place an ad in the Yellow Pages
> - Internet – have a lead generation-based web site
>
> **Where can my niche be found easily?**
>
> **At Work:**
> - Sales letters
> - Postcards
> - Fliers
> - Fax broadcast
> - Telemarketing
>
> **What publications do they read?**
> - Trade Magazine A – classified advertising and/or display advertising
> - Trade Magazine B – classified advertising and/or display advertising

Do you see how you can build your lead generation tools specific to your niche?

This is an amazingly simple approach but very few people apply the same logic when choosing their lead generation tools!

How to decide if you should use irresistible offers up-front or later in the sales process

In the last XBS Module we showed you how to create irresistible offers. In **every single case** you'd use your irresistible offer as part of your lead generation strategy.

Why?

Because your irresistible offer is the one thing that's going to attract your potential clients or customers to you in vast numbers.

Remember we identified 3 fabulous irresistible offers you can use…

> **3 Great Irresistible Offers That Always Work for Any Business Are…**
> - FREE Trials of Your Product/Service (the best offer)
> - FREE Special Reports (another favorite of ours)
> - FREE Additional Products/Services

Just make sure you've done your 'homework' and you've chosen your irresistible offer.

Next, we're going to explain how you multiply your response once you've chosen your lead generation tools and your irresistible offer…

The brilliant strategy that will make everything you do at least 10 times more effective

What we're about to reveal to you is something we rarely discuss with people.

It's what we call 'Laser Beam Focus.' Here's what we mean…

Laser Beam Focus – What's it all about?

To get the best possible results with all your advertising and marketing you must be laser focused on what each element in your sales process has to achieve for you.

Unfortunately, many people get confused and try to achieve more than one main objective with each of their marketing elements.

For example, …

Let's say you send a two-page sales letter to your prospects. The main objective is to generate qualified leads. You're using a Special Report as the "Irresistible Offer.'

That's easy enough to understand. But here's where most people go wrong…

Remember the main objective is to get qualified leads using the Special Report. That means you need to completely focus on the Special Report and explain why your prospects should respond. That's all that matters.

What most people do is lose this 'Laser Beam Focus' and try to achieve several things at once. They try to get an appointment, get the prospect to phone, and the Special Report is almost incidental. By using this 'scatter-gun' approach you significantly reduce response. Fewer responses mean fewer sales.

In effect what we're saying is that the tools and Tactics you use (not just in lead generation) must concentrate heavily on achieving the required outcome…

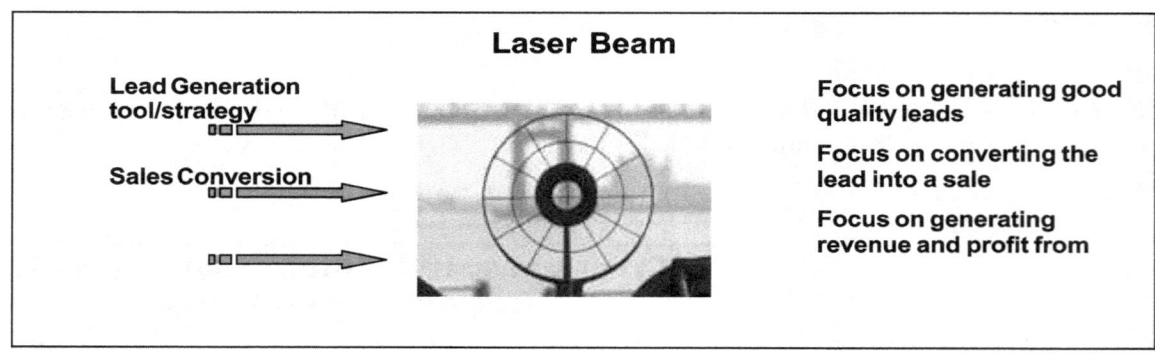

Don't confuse the issue. Confusion in the mind of your prospect spells NO ACTION.

The ad below shows one of Steve's lead generation ads. Notice how laser focused he is on getting accountants to request his free Special Report…

> **FREE *Report For Accountants Reveals The Secrets Of...***
>
> ## "How To Get A Constant Stream Of New Clients And More Fee Income From Existing Clients In 36 Days Or Less - Guaranteed"
>
> **For The Good Accountants Who Should Be Making More Money Than They Are...**
>
> Are you frustrated, unhappy, maybe even disgusted with the growth of your accountancy practice? Do you work all hours, but have little to show for it? Would you be delighted to do less work, especially less hard work, but make more money?
>
> If so, my FREE Special Report for accountants will help.
>
> **Being A Brilliant Accountant Counts For Very Little**
>
> Consider this... Even the best accountant in the world will go broke without a constant stream of new clients and more income from existing clients. It's that simple.
>
> The sad truth is most people rarely achieve just one of these things, never mind both of them.
>
> **What's The "Secret" Ingredient?**
>
> It's a familiar story, yet the key to your success is NOT to improve your expertise or even the service levels of your staff. No. The key is for you to become a sales and marketing whiz. That's right you heard me right - And yes - you can do it! Here's the proof...
>
> *"Thanks to your 'secret' sales and marketing approach, we have acquired 76 new clients and are averaging 6 new clients per month. This will generate approx £418,000 fee income over the next 5 years. Our average fee income has jumped from £850 to over £1,100."*
>
> **Rowena Barnwell**, Partner - Barnwell Brewin, Ashby de la Zouch, Leics
>
> **FREE Report Shows You How...**
>
> My FREE report titled, *"High Profit Secrets: How To Get A Constant Stream Of New Clients And More Fee Income From Existing Clients"* has all the answers. Inside this exciting report you'll discover...
>
> 1. The **vital ingredients** that guarantee your success, and using them in a simple and powerful growth system
> 2. How to use the three "**Success Keys**" to skyrocket your sales and profits
> 3. How to use the four "**Income Stream Generators**" to catapult your practice forward
> 4. How **dozens** of the best and mostly secret practice growth strategies are actually FREE to use. I've identified 67 of them!
> 5. How a simple 6 stage "**Selling Without Fear Sales Appointment**" can transform your client acquisitions
> 6. And many more **secrets** revealed
>
> **Get Your FREE Copy Right Now**
>
> **TO GET YOUR FREE COPY** of this exciting report, call my **free recorded message** (24 hours) on **0808 1449797**. Alternatively complete the coupon and post it back to me at the address below.
>
> ☐ **Yes!** Please send me your FREE Special Report. I want to discover the proven practice growth secrets
>
> First Name: _____
> Surname: _____
> Company: _____
> Address: _____
> Tel: _____
>
> Send To: Hackney Marketing Ltd,
> FREEPOST MID 18761, LEICESTER
> LE3 2ZJ. Tel: 0116 239 4433

Do you understand why this is so important? Whatever lead generation tools you choose you must be completely focused on your irresistible offer. You want people to receive the offer so you must focus everything on achieving this objective.

Do this and you will multiply the success of everything you do. (Notice laser beam focus applies to 'Sales Conversion' and 'Maximizing Profit from Existing Customers' as well as 'Lead Generation').

Now you have these 3 simples 'lead generation Tactics' combined together, you're ready to select your lead generation tools and apply them successfully to your niche or target market. That's what you'll do very shortly!

Module 12

Setting Your Objectives To Give You Direction

Creating objectives to give you a sense of tremendous satisfaction and to help drive your business forward

Introduction

We don't want to go into too much detail regarding setting your objectives. All we will say is you should spend some time thinking about what you want out of your business.

A good first step is trying to imagine how your business will look when it's **'finished.'** For example, in 3 or 5 years' time how many staff will you have? What services will you be selling? How many clients will you have?

This gives you somewhere to **aim**.

Now think about what you want to achieve in the next 12 months, 3 years, and 5 years. Try to be as specific as possible.

Don't just think about turnover and profit. Do you want to increase the number of offices you have? What about different locations, areas, and countries even?

Also think about your **personal** objectives. Do you want to spend less time in your business (one of the main reasons you're reading this program)? When are you planning on retiring? What's your exit strategy? What do you need to do to either sell the business or pass it on?

All these issues are important for you to think about. However, if you spend the time to think about your objectives, you'll achieve them and you'll achieve them much quicker.

One final note on objectives. It is much better to set your sights **high** rather than low. You may not reach your objectives ultimately, but the steps you take will be much greater than if you'd set lower and easier objectives.

Once you've decided on your objectives write them down. Keep referring back to your objectives periodically, to see how you're doing. And refine them if necessary.

To help you get started, your first objective should be to follow this program – page by page – step by step and use the Tactics immediately in your business!

Module 13

Budgeting

How to set your initial lead generation budget, and why you'll never need to budget in the future

Introduction

Have you ever budgeted your lead generation program? Don't worry if you haven't — we'd actually be surprised if you had.

What we're about to explain may surprise you, but it is the only way to approach this whole subject of, "How much money should I devote to lead generation?"

First, we're going to assume one thing. We're going to assume that you've never recorded the results of any lead generation you've done in the past. If you have taken accurate records, please stay with me because this is still important to you.

Without any past record you are starting 'blind.' You've got no data to suggest you'll get X new leads and Y clients
— resulting in Z profit if you do a, b, or c. Therefore, what you must do initially is set an 'Interim Lead Generation Budget.'

We call it an **Interim Lead Generation Budget** because you'll only use it for a few short months — maybe even weeks.

There are several ways to do this, but the most effective and logical is to look at your bank statement, cash flow and balance sheet and set an amount you can comfortably afford.

Don't over commit yourself. There really isn't any need. You'll soon find out that many successful Lead Generation Tools cost very little to use Low or no cost). Also, here's a word of advice you should adhere to…

> Always look at the worst-case scenario when using your Lead Generation Tools. If the worst-case scenario means you're going to lose money — don't go ahead. Don't say to yourself, "If I get 5%, I'll get X leads and Y clients and Z profit (we've done this in the past to our cost!).
>
> The chances are you won't meet your expectations and you could lose hundreds or even worse thousands of Rands. We've learned this the hard way — don't you do it too!

Don't forget you're only 'setting' this interim lead generation budget for now. You will not need to do it after a couple of months.

Here's why...

Once you know what works and what doesn't and how much profit each Lead Generation Tool brings, you can simply activate the tools repeatedly, or until they stop making a profit for you. It really is that simple.

> **Please Note:**
>
> **Listen carefully. The success of Each Lead Generation Tool you use will vary – quite considerably. That's why you need to record your results. The key is to improve or drop unprofitable tools and keep the profitable ones.**
>
> **But don't make this common mistake...**
>
> **Don't stop using a Lead Generation Tool because it isn't as profitable as another.**
>
> **The key is this...**
>
> **If it makes you money keep running it. In fact, do more of it.**
>
> **Does that make sense? Remember it's all about profit!**
>
> **Even if you get 'bored' with it don't stop doing it. Unfortunately, many people do – to their cost!**

There is however something **else** you need to be aware of (and take into account when setting your Interim Budget)
– and this is a real big strategy that will give you even more success.

It's what we call 'Cost of Client Acquisition.' We discussed it earlier. **You should refer back to this right now to jog your memory again (Module 10).**

If you remember, cost of client acquisition is the amount of money you are prepared to spend on lead generation to get a new client or customer. It ties in 'Lifetime Customer Value' and considers the profitability of the customer over the duration of the relationship they have with you.

Here's how to calculate your Interim Budget...

Let's take the following hypothetical (but realistic) figures...

Financial Item	Amount
First Order Value	R500.00
Gross Margin	50%
Gross Profit	R250.00
Orders Per Year	2
Average Lifetime	5 years
Lifetime Customer Value	R2,500

With these figures you can now look at how much you're prepared to spend to get a customer (cost of client acquisition) and set your interim budget…

> **Please Note:**
> We've obviously kept these figures simple and haven't included any cash flow forecasts etc. You should do this to help you reach a sensible and affordable Interim Budget figure.

Financial Item	Amount
First Order Value	R500.00
Gross Margin	50%
Gross Profit	R250.00
Cost Of Client Acquisition	R100.00
Profit on first order	R150.00

In this example we've taken the Cost of Client Acquisition at R100. This still leaves a profit on the first sale (but of course you can increase or decrease this amount depending on your circumstances).

Remember though, the more you spend to get a customer — the more customers you'll get!

Okay, so now let's look at how we calculate your Interim Budget...

1. The first thing to remember (as we mentioned earlier) is you need to be pessimistic when looking at the success of your Lead Generation Tools. It's better to under-estimate at this stage.

2. You'll shortly be choosing your Lead Generation Tools. Of course, many are low or no-cost tools, but some are more 'expensive' than others (remember if a lead generation tool makes you money it doesn't cost).

3. You need to do the following calculation for each individual lead generation tool. You can then assess its viability...

So, let's say one of your chosen lead generation tools is Yellow Pages advertising. It costs you R2,500 to place a 'double 3/8's column ad.' Let's look at the viability of using this tool...

Financial Item	Amount
Cost of Tool	R2,500.00
No. of customers required to break even on first order	10 (R2,500 divided by R250 gross profit)
No. of customers required to break even over lifetime	1 (R2,500 divided by R2,500 lifetime customer value)
Cost Of Client Acquisition	R100.00
Number of customers required to get cost of acquisition to R100	25 (R2,500 divided by R100 cost of customer acquisition)
No. of clients required per month	2
Current sales conversion percentage (number of leads that convert into customers)	25%
No. of leads required to get 25 customers	100
No. of leads per month required	8-9

Now you've painted a picture of what you need to achieve to at least break even. (You'll be working on your sales conversion soon but go with the figure you have at the moment).

In this example you'd have to say that Yellow Pages would be a good tool to use particularly when you consider you can pay for the ad over 6-10 months. In fact, Yellow Pages is often a PARTICULARLY good lead generation tool to use for many businesses.

Do you see how this works? Simply run each Lead Generation Tool through this same calculation and you'll be able to realistically evaluate which tools will be best for you to use.

You can then total the costs required and set your interim marketing budget.

Then once you start collecting the results from each tool, you'll be able to assess the good from the bad. Those that make a profit should be ramped up and used more often. Those that lose you money should be improved (to get them into profit) or dropped entirely.

And since you know which tools are profitable you don't actually have to set a budget in the future. You'll know if you spend RX, you'll always get R8X (or whatever), so as long as you keep a close eye on your cash flow, budgeting just isn't required.

Module 14

Selecting Your Lead Generation Tools

Choosing your lead generation tools and putting in place your 'Marketing Activity Plan'

Introduction

You've already come a long way. You're now fully prepared to launch a series of lead generation tools to bring you multiple streams of income.

Remember, each lead generation tool is capable of generating you many leads, which will in turn result in sales and new clients or customers for your business.

We're now going to take you through the simple stages of selecting the 'perfect' Lead Generation Tools for your business, and how you go about launching, improving and getting the best possible result for the least cost. How does that sound?

STEP 1: Go back to XBS Module 11 and re-read <u>HOW</u> to choose the best lead generation tools for your business

This is particularly important. You won't have ever selected your lead Generation Tools like this before, and using this strategy ensures your choice of Lead generation Tools is easier and more effective!

> **Please Note:**
>
> If you've been monitoring the success (or failure) of the Lead Generation Tools you've been using over the past, you MUST keep the ones that have been making you money. Do NOT drop these. Just add other tools to your list.
>
> Plus… we'll shortly be showing you how you can improve your existing successful Lead Generation Tools!

STEP 2: Turn to Manual 3 (If purchased R5000) 'The Quantum 133 Tactics & Action Points That Can Revolutionize Your Business'

Read the introductory text on how to use the book. At this stage only look at the section that concentrates on 'Lead Generation.' By combining what you learned in Module 11 with this reference book, you'll be able to choose a raft of fantastic Lead Generation Tools for your business.

STEP 3: Prioritizing Your Lead Generation Tools

The next step having selected your Lead Generation Tools is to prioritize them in the order you want to activate them.

- Remember you're **not** going to be able to activate all your Lead Generation Tools together. Others such as Yellow Pages advertising only needs to be activated when your local directory requires your ad. This could be at any point during the year!

- Simply go through your selected Lead Generation Tools and put them in **order** of priority. Of course, some will be easier to implement than others, and you'll be able to activate several at once.

- You also need to now take a look at your 'Interim Marketing Budget' (XBS Module 13) to help you prioritize and plan your way ahead.

- Now write the list of Lead Generation Tools down. You are now well on the way to developing your Lead Generation System.

    You should now have a list similar to the one below...

Selected Lead Generation Tools:
- Fax broadcast
- Special reports
- Direct Mail/Sales letters
- Press releases
- Seminars
- Newsletter
- Free consultations
- Networking
- Yellow Pages advertising
- Web site

STEP 4: Person responsibility

There are some Lead Generation Tools you'll want to **concentrate** on yourself. Others may be given to other people in your company. Others may be outsourced.

Of course, this is up to you, but what you must do – and this is especially important, is to make a person responsible (or a third-party company) to each Lead Generation Tool. By doing this you are giving 'ownership' to this particular person, which ensures the task **will** be completed by the time specified.

STEP 5: Timing

Now simply decide **when** you are going to launch each Lead Generation Tool. Some may be used more than once (and remember they should be used repeatedly as long as you are making a profit). Just build this into your schedule.

STEP 6: Creating Each Lead Generation Tool

In fairness this is the 'hardest' part of the XBS Program for you. The good news is that we've made it very easy for you to create powerful and very profitable Lead Generation Tools.

How can we do that since all lead generation tools are different?

It's because all your lead generation tools require sales-based copywriting to ensure you get the desired response. Remember, earlier we talked about 'Laser Beam Focus,' where each lead generation tool has a fixed objective? You then apply the Lead Generation Tool to get the desired response. This in 99% of cases is down to simple but amazingly effective copywriting Tactics.

As you know part of the XBS Program includes our Step-By-Step system for creating profit generating direct mail (sales letters, postcards, leaflets, inserts, etc), adverts (magazine advertising, trade magazine advertising, classified advertising etc), and all other Tools that are written or spoken.

All you need to do after selecting your Lead Generation Tools is to go through the simple steps in these Systems, and within no time you'll have created very powerful marketing tools generating more sales and profits than you ever thought possible.

STEP 7: Activate Your Lead Generation System

That's it. You've done it. You've created your first Lead Generation System. Didn't we tell you it was going to be easy!

Your system is easy to follow, easy to change, and easy to adapt. Once you start using your Lead Generation System, you'll soon be generating high quality leads from your targeted prospects.

The next stage of the process is to **TEST** each marketing tool. We test to ensure each Lead Generation Tool is performing at its optimum (i.e. best results for the least cost). This is what we'll cover next.

Module 15

How To Multiply The Results Of Your Lead Generation Super System

Testing is the simple way to get the best possible results for the least time, effort, and cost

Introduction

In this section we're going to show you how you can massively **increase** your success when you activate your Lead Generation System.

This technique is often talked about but **rarely** used. Yet it is the one thing that can increase your success tenfold or even more, literally overnight.

What are we talking about?

Testing!

Here's what advertising legend John Caples said...

> "I have seen one advertisement sell 19 times as much goods as another."

This result was achieved through testing!

Can you remember way back when we talked about recording your results? There is one question you must always ask when the lead comes in – "Where did you hear about us?"

This one simple question enables you to monitor how well your Lead Generation Tools are performing in terms of the leads and enquiries they generate. That's why you **must** ask this question – many people don't!

> **Please Note:**
>
> Often when you use our Lead Generation Tools, the lead is generated <u>without</u> the prospect having to talk directly to you. For example, you'll use fax back forms, reply forms, and coupons. In these instances, you'll instantly know where the lead has come from, as long as you follow our advice on 'coding' your forms and ads.
>
> 'Coding' is quite easy and is explained in detail in Profusion System Manual 4.

Having identified which Lead Generation Tool generated the lead you can then follow your sales conversion system and accurately monitor whether the lead turned into a client or customer or not. We can then measure the sales and profits generated (or loss) from that lead assuming it turns into a client or customer.

Do you see what you are doing here? You are making all your lead generation tools ACCOUNTABLE.

And you must do this.

You must be able to determine how well each Lead Generation tool is **performing** for you. By doing this you can then test certain things to see what effect the test has on response and income raised.

Of course, this monitoring is simplified greatly by using a contact management database…

> **Using A Contact Management Database To Systemize Your Whole Lead Generation And Marketing Systems**
>
> Okay you've done **90%** of the work that is going to make you more successful than you could imagine. But how do you streamline the process?
>
> All you need to do is buy an "off the shelf" contact management package that simply facilitates the whole XBS Programme.
>
> We recommend 'Goldmine' and 'ACT.'
>
> Both these companies offer free one-month trials. You can download a trail version by pointing your browser at the following web addresses…
>
> **Goldmine**
>
> \>\> http://www.frontrange.com
>
> **ACT**
>
> \>\> http://www.act.com
>
> Of course, you may already have a database package that will achieve the necessary tasks.
>
> At the very least your database package needs to be able to…
>
> - Quickly and easily allow you to enter what type of Lead Generation Tool produced the lead
> - Quickly and easily allow you to track all your Lead Generation Tools from lead to sale to determine the profitability of each tool

> - Quickly and easily search for specific people and companies.
> - Be able to select one or more companies or people at once (mail merge).
> - Allow you to set specific follow up calls, letters, and meetings.
> - Automatically record a contact "history" for each record.
> - Hold relevant data about each person / company.
> - Be able to conduct searches on the data depending on certain characteristics. For example, you may want to write to all people in your database who are Lawyers with 5 or more employees, in a certain postcode area.
>
> We're not going to explain all the **reasons** why you should use this software or how to use it – that's for the experts – not us. Just accept what we're saying and invest a couple of hundred Rands in the Goldmine or ACT software.

Okay, so you've activated your Lead Generation Tools, and you've carefully monitored the results. Now is the time to start testing. Here's what to do…

STEP 1 – Test ONE of the following components

There are many things you can test, but the following list includes the components that will give you the quickest and largest increases in success…

- Your list (database of prospects, or the publications you advertise in)
- Your offer
- Your headline
- Your price

On average by testing each of these components you can expect to achieve the following increases in success…

- Your list   400%
- Your offer   300%
- Your headline 200%
- Your price anything is possible!

If you test all components separately you could get a combined increase in response of over 900% – and this doesn't include the difference in pricing tests.

So instead of getting a 1% response you could get over 9% from the same time, effort, and cost.

Do you see why testing is so important to you? And these figures we've used are conservative!

Let us give you some quick examples, just in case you're not convinced…

List – Test 1

On our instruction a software training company tested 3 different lists – IT Training Masterfile, EMAP Computing, and Training Information Network Ltd. Incidentally all these lists are good lists.

IT Training Masterfile outperformed the worst list by 390% - that's nearly 4 times better!

Just think the business hadn't tested these lists. They may have got lucky and chose to use the IT Training Masterfile in the first place. But what if they hadn't? Their results would have been reduced considerably.

List – Test 2

We recently tested two respected lists – Thomson Directories and the Sales Manager Business Database.

The difference in response was 64%. Okay we know this is not a massive difference but just look at the effect – one list generated 46 enquiries and the other produced 75 enquiries. That's a big increase!

Offer – Test 1

A human resources business tested the offer of a FREE Consultancy against a Free Special Report. The Special Report was an astonishing 1200% better. For the same time, effort, and cost, the Special Report produced a result 12 times better – **wow!**

Offer – Test 2

Another business on our instruction tested the offers – 2 for 1 and Half Price. Yes, they are both the same in terms of the benefit to the client, but Half Price was 165% better!

Headline – Test 1

A business tested these two headlines we wrote for them…

"If There Was A Proven Method That Guaranteed To Grow Your Key Accounts, And Reduced The Risk Of Losing Them, <u>Without</u> Any Financial Risk Or Penalty, Would You Be Interested?"

…and…

"Do You Know How Long It Could Take To Lose One Of Your Key Accounts? It Could Be A Lot Quicker Than You Ever Thought, And There's Nothing In Your Power To Prevent It. That Is Until Now"

Both these headlines are good headlines selling the same service. In both cases the rest of the letter was exactly the same.

The first headline was surprisingly 440% better!

Headline – Test 2

Again, these two headlines were tested against one another without any changes to the rest of the letter…

How You Can Become The <u>Lowest</u> Cost Producer In Your Market Place

…and…

How To Multiply The Profits Of Your Manufacturing Business

The top headline was a staggering 725% better!

Price – Test 1

On our instruction, one management consultant tested his service at two different price points R25,000 and R50,000. Guess what?

There was no difference in response. His prospects bought his service at the higher price <u>without</u> a drop in response. This means he literally doubled his fee income overnight. If he hadn't tested his price, he would be wasting thousands of Rands.

Clearly in this example the client was selling such a fantastic service for far less than it was worth (remember it's all about the value and not the price!), but this is common in our experience.

STEP 2 – Only test one component at a time

This is important. You must only change one component at a time. If you change 2 or more simultaneously, you'll never know which change was most successful (or otherwise).

STEP 3 – Record all your results – good and bad

It is often said you learn more from your mistakes than you do of your successes. This is true, but when you test there is never a bad outcome. Even if your test doesn't result in an increase in response and profit, you will have learned a great deal.

Record everything religiously! Please see the next page for a result sheet you can use.

STEP 4 – Keep testing

You should be continually testing. Don't stop at doing one headline test. Keep testing different headlines against your most successful one.

Can you see what you could be **missing** out on by not testing? And it really is extremely easy to test.

Please take on board what we've just said. Test, test, test, and you'll increase your sales, income, and profits quicker than you ever thought possible.

ADVERTISING AND PROMOTION RESULTS ANALYSIS

A	Date the ad or promotion ran, or letters sent out		
B	Promotion Name		
C	Ad Code		
D	Targeted Market		
E	No. of Letters Sent		
F	No. of Responses and Percent of Response	Number	Percentage
G	Number of Sales		
H	Sale Value *Price per unit_____ x no. of sales:_____*		
I	Less Cost of Fulfillment *(Packaging, product, shipping, etc.)*		
J	Less Cost of Promotion or Ad • No. of letters:_____ x stamp/letter:_____= • Printing of letters/unit:_____ = • Envelopes:_____ x no. of letters:_____= • Stuffing envelopes (labor):_____ = • Grabber/unit:_____ x no. of letters:_____=		
K	Net Profit (Loss) on Promotion *(Total Sales less cost of promotion and cost of fulfillment)*		
L	Profit-Loss per R spent on promotion *(Divide net profit-loss by cost of promotion)*		

Comments:

Conclusion

That's it. Your Lead Generation System is complete. Don't underestimate what you've achieved. Your system will be an amazingly powerful growth tool.

When you combine it with your 'Sales Conversion' and 'Maximizing Profit From Existing Customers' Systems you won't recognize your business in a few short weeks/months.

Consider buying the Second Manual